INDIA

LONDON | NEW YORK
STUDIO VISTA | THE VIKING PRESS
© STUDIO VISTA LTD 1961

Reprinted 1965
The original edition was published by Editions du Seuil, Paris

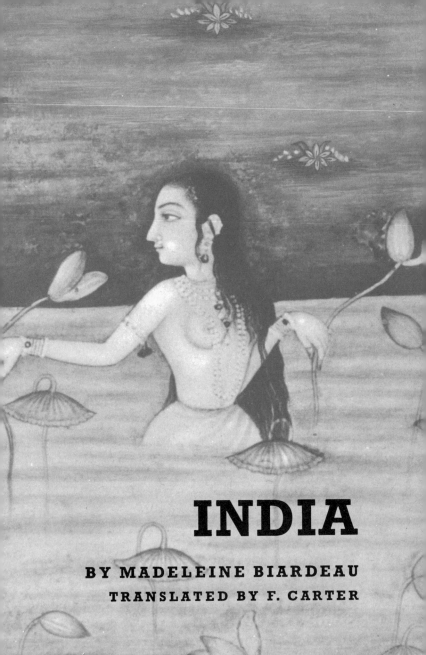

INDIA

BY MADELEINE BIARDEAU
TRANSLATED BY F. CARTER

Anjali

WHY IS IT that, for some years now, no one in this country or anywhere else speaks of India without raising his eyes to heaven? India, the country of the spirit, the hospitable sanctuary of all religions, consenting to call God by every name man has bestowed on Him; land of indefatigable meditation which does not give up its pursuit of the divine until it has attained its end, complete identification with the Absolute; so that it is not always easy to remember that in India men are made of flesh and blood and that by and large their daily life is as uneventful as our own. So much so that Westerners arrive on Indian soil in their hundreds more or less persuaded that they will find Enlightenment round the corner. Whereas in fact what they encounter is India, with its dirt, poverty, discomfort; and they never cease reciting what makes this country one of the most backward. Life must be impossible here.

And what of Indian culture? What of the unique and universal human face presented by the peasant or the Brahman of the land of Bharat? They lightly pass that over. Well, this is precisely what I want to talk about, in relation to the new complexity introduced by a modern economy. So I hope my Indian readers will forgive me if, in doing so, I occasionally bring to light some less pleasing aspect of their country.

Land of the Bharatas

I LAND AT BOMBAY. As on my first visit the ravens are the first living things to greet me; they are an invariable feature of the Indian scene, as their croaking is the invariable accompaniment to the background music of Indian life. Are they birds of ill omen here? The Indians do not care for them much, but with what delight they hail them, as the symbol of their country, on their return from abroad!

I hear in my first talk with old friends: France has at last realized that Pondicherry must be Indian, and in Goa Portugal has realised too.

This foreign enclave in India, this out-of-date remnant of bygone glory, is a thorn in the flesh to every Indian. Their country is amputated; Goa is their Alsace-Lorraine, even though they have not yet fought for it. India must be reintegrated; India must be for the Indians, India, India . . . India is an independent Republic, one and indivisible.

And now the second topic of conversation with these same Maratha friends who live in Bombay: it is a disgrace, they are trying to deprive us of our capital. Bombay belongs to the Maharashtrians, Bombay cannot be Gujarat territory. Here the situation becomes a little intricate: the state of Bombay, where both Gujarati and Marathi are spoken, is divided into two regions, or what amounted to two regions before the Government decided to unite them.

For the most part industrial and big trading interests are in the hands of the Gujaratis; the workers and small people in general are Maharashtrians; for which reason the Communists are given to understand that a Maratha Bombay would not do because it would quickly lead to Communist local government. The Maharashtrians, quite simply and in general, look upon Bombay as their natural capital. Thus there are demonstrations, disturbances, strikes, and railway communications are cut. It has not yet come to civil strife, but it is not far off it. And, if it comes to that, would it be civil strife or a war between foreign states? One cannot help asking, so completely in the heat of controversy have the Maharashtrians and Gujaratis all at once forgotten their common motherland.

There you have India in a nutshell: in relation to the foreigner, and one moreover who occupies a corner of the country, the Indian is not merely a patriot but a nationalist; there is as little question for him about Kashmir as about Goa. He feels that he belongs to a young nation whose very existence, and not only its independence, are of recent date; and he therefore as readily adopts a militant attitude in defence of his own country as in defence of any other young nation. But when it comes to home questions he is first and foremost Tamil or Malayalam or Maratha or Bengali or Punjabi, which designations themselves cover wide divisions.

There is no way of understanding the situation without reference to history. It hardly helps towards an understanding of a modern Western state today to know that its political unity spread outwards from some central region. If certain parts of the British Isles, for example, have not entirely lost their original traits, these have become blurred, as have their local traditional culture. Or, to take France, is there a Burgundian alive today who would demand special legislation for Burgundy by reference to Charles the Bold? It is true that in this case he would not have the help of a distinctive Burgundian language of his own which segregated him. But India is divided by its languages and even by its groups of languages which cover profound ethnic differences: the Aryans of the North, the Dravidians of the South, not to mention the so-called aboriginal, pre-Dravidian, tribes which, untouched by the main currents of Hindu culture and, to some extent, of history, are scattered over the whole of India. At first glance, the vast territory of the sub-continent appears to have nothing but a geographical unity; the human divisions are immediately obvious. Language brings one back to history and history itself is incorporated in that of language.

If one takes a bird's-eye view of the dark confusion of dynastic struggles, of the wars of territorial conquest, paying at least as much attention to cultural trends as to political history, one can plainly trace all the components of the Indian nation of today and of present-day Indian national consciousness, with its conflicts and apparent contradictions. People are Marathi, Bengali, or Tamil because the written memorials in those languages, the stone monuments left by earlier centuries, bear witness to the past greatness of their region. It may have been short-lived, or belated, but it was achieved in defiance of adjacent people, that is to say, of enemies; it had its heroes who still live in popular memory, and perhaps the national consciousness of a Marathi was all but reduced to what is today no more than his 'regional' consciousness.

Land of the Bharatas

In fact, there is not an educated Indian – except in the extreme South – who forgets the existence of the great Indian Empires and who does not recognize in them a special significance.

It is worth pausing here for a moment. No one confuses the purely Maratha glory of a Sivaji (17th century) or the purely Dravidian one of the kingdom of Vijayanagar (14th to 17th centuries) with the all-powerful Emperors *Cakravartins,* the Universal Sovereigns – who emerged three times in India's history: first the Mauryas, at the dawn of that history, with great Asoka (3rd century B.C.), then the Guptas (4th to 6th centuries A.D.) whose power and brilliance King Harsha-vardhana maintained until the 7th century, and finally the 'Great Mughals', of whom present-day Indian memory retains practically none but Akbar (second half of the 16th century).

Akbar and his horse

Land of the Bharatas

The two former empires were built up to stem the 'barbarian' invaders (including the Greeks!) from the north-west, while the third signalised the permanent settling of new invaders on Indian soil. None of them ever united the entire sub-continent under their domination, and yet it is they whom the Indian invokes today in tracing the origins of his nation in history, despite interruptions, despite the British interlude. In his eyes the great emperors are the main architects of true Indian unity, the unity of culture, and the reign of each one of them coincided with a more illustrious blaze of that culture.

The Union Government, immediately after independence, chose Asoka's Sarnath Lion pillar, though without its Buddhistic wheel, as the emblem of the Indian Union. Apart from the fact that the pillars left by Asoka are the most ancient stone monuments in India, they speak of the glory of an emperor who in his day was undoubtedly the greatest prince reigning on the face of the earth. But more than that: they conjure up an entire programme that is in the purest Indian tradition.

It is an interesting thing that while Asoka was a notable convert to Buddhism, the Gupta emperors were Hindus and Akbar was a Muslim. But in every case, the same religious tolerance was practised. Although Asoka's conversion put the stamp of approval on Buddhism in India, it is striking that his famous edicts engraved on stone do not preach the truths of Buddhism itself so much as universal tolerance and peace. Akbar surrounded himself with the followers of every known religion, including two Jesuits, whom he enjoyed hearing in disputation. Under the Hindu dynasty of the Guptas, a Buddhist revival was witnessed, peopling with meditators the caves abandoned after the Mauryas.

This spirit of tolerance or even, possibly syncretism was extended even to the invaders who ceaselessly, from the time of the Achaemenian Persians, poured into India over the Khaibar Pass. Petty 'barbarian' kings protected Sanskrit literature; none of them was converted to either Hinduism or Buddhism. India, on the other hand, was willing to learn from the intruders, from the Greeks to the Muslims. The presence of the latter in particular gave rise to strong syncretist trends whose influence can still be felt. It is not unusual to find the tombs of Muslim saints today tended and venerated by Hindus. And now, under the high patronage

of the Vice-President of the Indian Union, Dr. Sarvapalli Radhakrishnan, India is planning to call a conference of the great religions with the object, apparently, of finding their common denominator. There is no doubt a political motive behind this, but the fact remains that an ambition of this kind could be conceived only in India. As it is, a congress has been held every year for some time past to study the great religions, which has nothing to do with a congress for the study of the history of religion: I will not go so far as to say that all the participants give evidence of the same syncretism as Dr. Radhakrishnan.

The relative continuity of this tradition of tolerance explains perhaps to some extent the cultural unity of the sub-continent, even despite the wars which stand out as landmarks over the centuries. Buddhism spread right to the South where, in fact, the Hindu counter-offensive that was to eliminate it arose; Sanskrit, the Aryan tongue, originally confined to the North, gradually became the cultural language of the peninsula, and it grew increasingly difficult to trace strictly Dravidian culture, so much was it overlaid by Hinduism, which absorbed everything it could assimilate. When the Muslims embarked on their periodic incursions and destructions in the 11th century, the South had already assured the relief of the North, and the greatest philosophers of Hindu India and of Sanskrit expression, after the 7th century, were in all probability Dravidian, judging by their place of origin.

Myths

India's culture, in essence Hindu, was already developed, and its basic writings established, when the Mauryan empire came into being. It is not contemporary with India, historically speaking, as a nation; its origins are lost in myth. There is quite a lot of information about periods prior to the Mauryan dynasty; it is known in general that the Aryans came from the north-west and gradually forged their way eastwards, probably driving back a Dravidian population; it is known that India or part of India had had an earlier civilization, urban and mercantile, at any rate in the Indus Valley (Mohenjo Daro and Harappa), and that the village culture it had introduced was already an advance over the nomadic life that had been known before. But the scripts are so far indecipherable, trying to establish dates is a real brain-teaser and it has needed the combined efforts of European scholars to bring some sort of order and disentangle history from myth in the Vedas and Brahmanas, the most ancient texts to have come down to us, and the great epics of the *Mahabharata* and the *Ramayana;* even in more recent times, the genealogical tables of the *Puranas* and the whole literature yield nothing but conflicting, confused and undated facts.

The Hindu, however, does not draw a sharp distinction between myth and history; to him Rama, the prince, first hero and then deity, is certainly a more real character than Asoka. Buddha means no more to him than an avatar of Vishnu, like Rama, like Krishna the shepherd-king of Vrindavana. Myth is more familiar to him on the whole: he has transformed the facts and clothed them in accordance with Hindu taste; miracles abound, gods and men mingle, and the first sovereigns found mythical dynasties. Rama, the hero of the *Ramayana,* is a prince of the sun dynasty. In this way

Râma

the very name of India used in the national anthem – Bharat – links the nation of today to one of its legendary princes, or rather to his descendants: Bharata himself belongs to the moon dynasty and, according to some legends, was the first Indian emperor. It was two branches of his descendants, the Kauravas and the Pandavas, who warred against each other in what was itself a half-mythical war, as recounted in the *Mahabharata*. For the average Indian these two epics are almost the only 'historical' sources. But history and historical evolution make little impression on him, or rather do not fall within his vision of the universe. Not that he denies that society has evolved, but each stage of its evolution – still today, for that matter, far from clear – is immediately 'eternalized', welded to a past too distant, vouched for by authorities too sacred to be thought of as something new. The Indian has been taught that his forefathers possessed scientific and technical knowledge superior in their day to any in the whole world; so much so, indeed, that he will assert on the evidence of some highly obscure script that India had aeroplanes two thousand years ago. These ancient treatises codify the contemporary state of knowledge in every field as though it were fixed for all time. In our countries in the West, every age has had some temptation to believe that it has reached a stage where knowledge can go no further, but it does at least retain a feeling for what has been accumulated, for stages past. Not so the Indian. For him all knowledge savours of eternity and, by that token, is sacred. If time plays any part at all it is a destructive one: learning and orthodoxy are on the decline, a sign that things are going to the bad in our Kali-yuga. The Indian divides the aeons of the world into ages *(yugas)* which progressively decline until absorbed again in Siva or in Vishnu, after which the cycle starts once more, and so on for eternity. Kali-yuga is the last, the worst, age. Even the avatars of Vishnu, periodically appearing to re-educate mankind, cannot effect much change in the cycle.

So the Hindu – the Indian – is not plagued by the sense that time is flying: this time will come again, in its own good time, without any need to worry about the present or the future. That represents a whole programme. Consequently, patience in this country is inexhaustible, and the Westerner who chafes against the leisurely pace and the slightest waste of time is met with ironical smiles, or even frank bursts of

laughter. It is not that Indians cannot hurry themselves — even under the tropical sun — but what is the use?

Thus, living eternally in the present and at present in eternity, the Indian has developed an exceedingly complex culture which, in terms of religion, is called Hinduism, and in social terms — inseparable from religion — is characterized by the caste system. In point of fact, the domination of the Brahmans, in the still mythical age when the Aryans could keep themselves pure, suffered severe setbacks: round about the 6th century B.C. Buddhism and Jainism emerged, not to mention materialist trends which were speedily smothered. However, Brahmanism increasingly assimilated the alien elements, including Buddhist ones, to become Hinduism. From the sacrificial and aristocratic religion that it had been, it was gradually transformed by meeting the strictly religious needs of the mass of the people. The strange pantheon of Veda was replaced by gods more human, more accessible to man's prayers. Siva and Vishnu in their multiple forms were worshipped in temples from about the 5th century, whereas the Brahmanical religion had no need of a permanent place of worship. Underlying all meanwhile was the Vedic current, reappearing from time to time, and the Vedas continued to be regarded as the most sacred texts of Hinduism; even if no one turns to them any longer, they remain self-revelatory: neither gods nor men could be powerful enough to bridge the human world and the beyond. Thus the Vedas are this 'beyond' made word (and not man). Very advanced sages have been able to hear them and have transmitted them in their present form to lesser men.

This was the culture already known to Asoka's empire in the 3rd century B.C., a culture which simultaneously extols love of life, submission to cosmic order and escape to an immeasurable Absolute. The Vedas, the Brahmanas, the Upanishads, the first rudiments of the epics, of the *Puranas,* and of philosophical reflections laid the groundwork of contemporary Brahmanism and future Hinduism. It was no longer a 'pure', Aryan, culture; not only did Buddhism and Jainism jolt it badly — and still do — but popular, Dravidian, even *munda* (aboriginal) elements were introduced, in the form of deities and magical practices, into the Vedas themselves. Hindu philosophical systems and Buddhist works had still to see the light of day or to be put into shape. But all the essentials were there, at the dawn of history, emerging in the course of long ages. Caste, too, was already in being, not in so rigid a form as it was to assume later, but no longer the simple Vedic division into four broad social groups. The Mauryas, as a matter of fact, were probably *sudras,* dedicated by birth to menial tasks rather than to sovereignty. As history progressed all that was done was to re-interpret the heritage of the past, define it, complicate it, bring it into line with new, extraneous elements, acceptable only in so far as they could be accommodated within an already established world outlook; Hindu philosophical literature is a literature of commentaries on exceedingly ancient and often highly obscure basic writings and, later, of commentaries on commentaries; so that additions may be made, but never subtractions.

At first, indeed, one is tempted to define Hinduism as an infinite capacity for assimilation. No religion remains alien to it; it can give its blessing to every faith, clothing it, of course, after its own fashion. It is syncretism incarnate, paradoxical as that may seem in the light of the Hindu's rigid orthodoxy, which is in no way affected for all that.

I referred to the calling of a conference of the great religions; nothing could be more logical by Hindu-Indian standards: no religion holds the truth, but each religion leads to salvation in its own way. But then, does not Hinduism contain the truth? Yes, it does, because it is above religions, it rises to the experience of the Absolute itself, to ultimate unity. The words inscribed by the Theosophical Society on the pediment of their world centre in Madras express a purely Hindu sentiment: 'No religion is greater than the Truth.' Hinduism, like theosophy, is on the side of truth.

The same attitude is discernible in other contexts: India is naturally anti-racialist; she fraternizes with every people in the world and above all with those of the underdeveloped countries. A few years ago, Dr. Radhakrishnan stayed in Kenya for a few days. An Indian paper was bold enough to comment on the cold reception the Africans accorded to the Indian Vice-President and to give the reason: Indians living in Kenya do not treat Africans as equals. All races are equal, all peoples are equal, but Hindus are slightly above them. And to this is added caste-consciousness which sets the Hindu apart, even in his own country. As early as the beginning of the 11th century the Muslim Al-Biruni noted uncomplimentarily: 'The Hindus believe that there is no country but their own, no nation like theirs, no kings like theirs, no religion like theirs, no learning like theirs ... If they travelled and mixed with other peoples they would quickly change their views, for their forebears were not as narrow-minded as the present generation.' After a period of expansion – Asoka's Buddhistic missions, the visits of Chinese Buddhist pilgrims, the trade and cultural relations between the southern kingdoms and the Far East, not to speak of relations with the Roman Empire – India withdrew into herself. Orthodoxy forbade crossing the ocean, leaving the frontiers of Bharata the only pure territory; so no further interest was taken in foreign countries, that is, countries other than those within the sub-continent where, however, Hindu culture perpetually travelled from north to south and from west to east. Ignorance about the rest of the world encouraged, even and most particularly under the Mughal occupation, a certain Hindu, not to say Indian, arrogance, whose vestiges we still find today. It is this which rallies the entire nation – with the Communists in the forefront – in support of the Nehru of Bandung, the V. K. Menon of the United Nations. So long as foreign policy is brilliant and glorious, there will never be more than a handful of people to criticize effectively any shortcomings in domestic policy.

Revival

How came such national pride to allow Europeans to establish themselves on Indian soil from the end of the 15th century onwards? And how, above all, was the British Empire in India possible, considering that the British themselves are such individualists? To explain this, a great many manoeuvres, a great many battles and betrayals would have to be described. Political anarchy is one explanation: India was so divided that she was incapable of resisting a powerful enemy. She positively helped him, insofar as the rajahs appealed for support against each other to the foreign East India Companies: the French, then mainly the English, not to mention the Portuguese, Dutch and Danish. Here more than anywhere else British policy was based on the principle of Divide and Rule, or at any rate on that of exploiting existing divisions.

Another explanation is to be found in the cultural degeneration of India at that time. She had waged such struggles against Islam, with which some had ended by coming to terms, that she was resting on her laurels. Hindu mentality, perceiving none but imminent dangers, did not appreciate the menace which the presence of the West held over her. And what, indeed, could have been done against that multitude of petty rulers who, far from being concerned about the lustre of Hindu culture, could see no further than the end of their thrones?

So for once history repeated itself: those who had made the Muslim invasion possible now allowed the British to establish themselves in India. But, by another repetition, the presence of the British, which was always to be felt as a foreign body

lodged in an organism, gave rise to a twofold reaction: at first the Hindus re-discovered their own spiritual values. As in the time of the Mughals, there were some who, coming in contact with a new culture, sought only to absorb its substance without losing any of their own. This was the aim of Brahmo-Samaj syncretism, founded and developed in Bengal in 1868 by Ram Mohan Roy who, incidentally, became an official of the East India Company. The Society, under its successive leaders – Debendranath Tagore (grandfather of the poet) and Keshab Chandra Sen – and, by way of constant splits, evolved something halfway between Vedism and Christianity. Ram Mohan Roy and Keshab Chandra Sen worshipped Christ, without in any way attempting to

become Christians; they wished to take the best from all religions. Debendranath Tagore, on the other hand, distrusted an imported Christianity and was concerned only with the question of national heritage. He was the Loisy of Hinduism, so to speak, in refusing to acknowledge the ultimate validity of the Vedas or of any other sacred text. The attempt to reach a compromise between East and West was pursued very much later, in the 20th century, on a philosophical basis, by Aurobindo Ghose who, though he had been an anti-British political agitator in Bengal, became the founder of an *asram* which is still very much alive in Pondicherry. Its content derives as much from Hindu tradition as from Hegel's and Bergson's philosophies. In its literary and artistic expression, the desire to combine Western and Indian culture was personified by Rabindranath Tagore, who with this end in view set up an international university at Santiniketan (Bengal).

The Ramakrishna Mission had an entirely different basis; it was not brought into being by either a favourable or a hostile reaction to the presence of the British, and it was less the outcome of the mystical experiences of Ramakrishna Paramahamsa than of the outlook of his disciple Swami Vivekananda, who was deeply impressed by the charitable institutions of Europe and America. It is an 'Indian Mission' in the sense in which we speak of England or the United States as a 'missionary country'. Vivekananda founded it to provide young Hindus with both a religious and a humanitarian training. Today the Ramakrishna Mission in India has a mainly practical function through its hospitals and social services, except, possibly, in the Calcutta area, where it had its beginnings.

At the other end of the scale the Arya-Samaj, organized in Bombay in 1875 by Dayanand Sarasvati, brought together those who, reacting against the foreigner, rehabilitated the values of Hindu orthodoxy. A kind of Hindu Protestantism, the Arya-Samaj preached a return to the Vedas, but the Vedas re-interpreted, and purged of accretions alien to its traditions. It did not quite succeed in its plan to set up *gurukuls:* novitiate schools where the young Hindu would receive orthodox instruction and at the same time a modern scientific education, though the *gurukul* at Kangri near Haridvar still takes male and female students today.

There was another form of European influence of which too few people are aware. Apart from these various movements, Hindus, generally Brahmans, set to work practically everywhere to study their own culture. They were conscious of their ignorance, of the disrepute into which Vedic studies had fallen and of the false scholarship of teaching children to recite the Vedas by heart until they were able to reel them off backwards, from the last word to the first. The meaning of the words no longer mattered. So they set themselves the task of restoring sense and spiritual content to what had become a mere jingle of words, but – and this is what was new – they borrowed from European methods of scholarship. In fact, at a time when Great Britain still thought of nothing but ransacking India and making the whole weight of her power felt, Sir William Jones founded the Asiatic Society of Bengal (1784), and translated the drama *Sakuntala* (1789) and the lawbook of Manu (posthumously published in 1794 as *Institutes of Hindoo Law*). It was again an Englishman, James Prinsep, who deciphered the Asoka inscriptions, one of the main sources of the history of his reign; while another Englishman, Charles Wilkins, translated the *Bhagavad Gita* ('Song of the Adorable One') in 1785. Grierson's *Linguistic Survey*, the *Archaeological Survey* established by Cunningham, and many others – Henry Colebrook, Horace Wilson, John Marshall – should be mentioned, not forgetting above all the *Gazetteers* and *Manuals* where, bit by bit, obscure British officials assembled an enormous mass of sociological and other information on castes and tribes. French Indologists were not far behind; could even be said to have started the ball rolling with the work of P. Pons on Indian philosophy in 1740, and his first catalogue of Sanskrit manuscripts (1739). Another Frenchman, Deguignes, explored the foreign sources of India's history – Chinese, Persian, Greek – and discovered that the Sandrokottos mentioned by the Greeks was none other than the Mauryan Emperor Chandragupta: * this being one of the rare landmarks we have in ancient Indian chronology. In short, Europeans restored to the Hindus a whole lost or hitherto unknown world. In this way, no less than by the systematic British exploitation of India, they helped towards the creation of Indian nationalism. It is no overstatement that the Commission which, in early 1957, toured India to revive the study of Sanskrit was the heir to the great European scholars.

The period of cultural revival was followed by the struggle for independence, waged on economic and political lines. The Indian National Congress was founded – by an Englishman – in 1885, but was little more at that time than a mouthpiece for a few new 'bourgeois' Indians to voice their grievances and aspirations. The real struggle began only at the end of the First World War, when the reforms proposed by the British Government led the National Congress to demand autonomy for the first time. Gandhi assumed leadership in the fight, less because he was convinced of the need for autonomy – he was not – than to stem a popular uprising. This state of affairs lasted until 1947. On August 15th in that year complete independence was proclaimed. There was a good deal of astonishment at this outcome,

pacifically reached, and the credit for it was attributed entirely to India or, rather, to Gandhi, the pacifist. Today it is only fair, in view of the independence of Ghana and of Malaya, to acknowledge British sagacity and skill. One should also give Nehru his due; for it cannot be denied that, when India achieved its independence in 1947, the immediate outlook was far from bright and the country stood on the verge of chaos. India had to accept the painful amputation of Pakistan (the very idea of which had been mooted only in 1940), whilst retaining 40 million Muslims and being inundated by waves of Hindu immigrants who refused to stay on Islamic soil. The British had laid down the frontiers – previously very flexible – on capricious and quite unjustifiable lines, if only to please the princes who had served the imperialist cause. Compare this with the partition of Indonesia after independence! On the abating of the first fevers and the ending of the appalling mutual massacres of Hindu and Muslim, Congress, with Nehru and Patel exercising an iron rule, achieved the unification of India. For this, of course, the decision of the Hindu Maharajah of Kashmir to opt for India had to be ratified, without enquiring too closely into the wishes of the Muslim population, whereas nobody asked for the (Muslim) Nizam of Hyderabad's views before sending Indian troops into his territory. Since the recent redrawing of the frontiers, the Nizam's State has been divided between those of Andhra and Mysore (Karnataka). The petty kings are so only in name now. They receive a pension which comes to an end when they die; and even that is beginning to be challenged here and there.

But who can wonder at wranglings over the States of the new federal Republic, proclaimed on January 30th, 1949, once the Constitution had been drafted? Naturally everyone felt that the neighbouring State was getting more from the Union Government. The State Legislative Assemblies tended to see problems only within the dimensions of their own frontiers. But for the first time they were thinking out these problems for themselves, taking responsibility for the whole. Power everywhere, including, until recently, in Kerala, is vested in national parties.

It is probably true to say that actually the Indian's national consciousness is not quite the same as ours; he certainly feels himself Indian in relation to the foreigner; but if he moves from one State to another he is no longer in his own

country because of the differences of language and customs,
even though the constant cultural basis may be the same.
So far as a matter of fact, he seldom leaves his own State,
but if new economic advances entail, as they are beginning
to do, some displacement of population and changes of
State, it will mean that the Indian will learn to know his
country – the land of Bharat – better; naturally he will
remain devoted to his native State – and why not? – but
he will go and live where his work requires him. The first
test of this will be the Indian Army, which is not on a State
basis. The soldiers – all regulars, as there is no conscription
– have marched from one end of India to the other and, on
principle, do not stay for more than two years in the same
garrison. Thus there is a wholesale mixing of men from
different states, which in no way hinders a vigorous social
interchange, very often with English as the only common
language.

But modern life, though it may mean the loss of many
legacies from the past, also demonstrates a definite unity
which is made up of something other than an imitation of
the West. I shall not speak of the classical arts, which
are practically non-existent in the India of today: the Indians
have an almost unbelievable incapacity nowadays for ap-
preciating the things we most admire in their country. Apart
from the Taj Mahal, which they only go to see by moon-
light, the beauty of their temples and of every other relic
of bygone art escapes them altogether. I gave up when I
was trying to explain to a Brahman engineer one day what
it was that I liked about the dancers on a bas-relief we
were looking at. He asked me very earnestly: 'But wouldn't
you prefer them if they were more lifelike?' 'If what were?'
'The dancers.' I could not summon up an answer. Very
definitely the Indians have not yet found their way back
to a past before the British and the Mughals. Young
painters too often go in for wild symbolism, when not just
imitating Western painting of the last half-century.

At the same time the main Indian languages, which are not
as numerous as is often made out, are or have become the
languages of culture. The novel in particular spreads this;
making allowance for the characteristics peculiar to each
language, it seems to me that one can recognize the affinity
between a Tamil and a Hindi work. Possibly the novelist
of the North has been more influenced by the West – if

Tolstoy can be taken as a true representative of Western culture – and his literary vein is more idealistic; but it is nevertheless an Indian voice; as for the Tamil, he may be Dravidian but he, too, is first and foremost Indian. The inspiration provided by the social scene is exploited by the one no less than by the other, and in the same manner; love stories are recounted in a similar setting. And this national

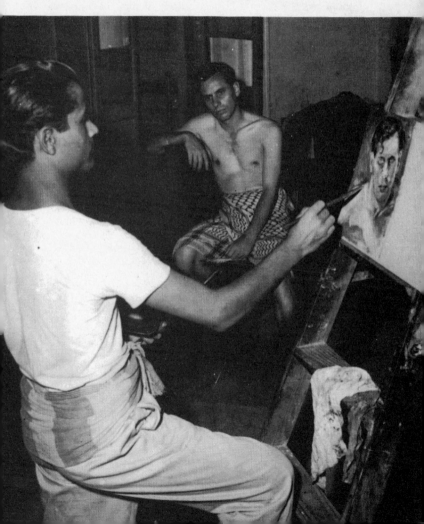

strain can be traced even in novelists who have elected English as their medium of expression. Mulk Raj Anand's *Coolie and Inquilab* (Revolution) by the Muslim Khwaja Ahmad Abbas have the same diction as Prem Chand's Hindi novel; these similarities being the more striking in that each lays emphasis upon different regional customs.

The most directly national art is undoubtedly the cinema. India has the second largest output of films in the world and yet, despite all efforts, has the utmost difficulty to export her reels. Poor technique is by no means the only reason; it is far more the whole approach: the way of treating the subject, the techniques of construction, the psychology of the characters and the style of acting make the Indian film a commodity for home consumption. If the Western public judged it by, for example, *Two Acres of Land*, they would be wrong. In spite of the indispensable lyrical passages and a certain sentimentality, this film has undoubtedly taken its cue from the West, in particular from the Italian school, in that it tries to be 'realist' and poetic at the same time. Most Indian films are very different: not inferior – which is nonsense, for how can we judge of the matter? – but different. Elements of mythological drama have been transposed into terms of cinema, even when treating of contemporary subjects. For example in the famous 'social dramas' the mother-in-law is as detestable as in our countries; the characters are conventionalized, lacking in psychological depth; the settings give no feeling of time or place; the story is often highly improbable; the acting, particularly by the women, is always too exaggerated for our taste and the sentimentality quite intolerable. But the Indian public cannot do without its cinema nowadays; Madras films go down as well in the North as do Bombay films in the South. Where people are slightly more educated and understand English they go to see the endless stream of Westerns that Hollywood pours into India even more lavishly than into Britain.

What would be needed to make Indian films as acceptable to our countries as are, for example, Japanese films? Perhaps, quite simply, that they find their own authentic idiom instead of giving us on the screen the equivalent of the most hideous modern religious prints. Despite myself, I am levelling judgments, and there is no getting away from the fact that we cannot take to these artless illustrations and sickly-sweet characters. There is, when all is said and done,

Satyajit Ray ▲

'Aparajito' ▼

a certain universality of taste which allows us to enjoy ancient Indian art and Japanese films of the most Japanese character. So perhaps, after all, it is permissible to pass judgment and to hope that contemporary India will recover its lost taste.

These national manifestations are only the expression – sometimes still a rather clumsy one – of a genuine Pan-Indian culture. Though Hinduism may be on the decline, it has none the less moulded consciousness and general attitudes through the ages, even affecting Indian Muslims and leaving its mark on Christian converts. Indian unity is made up of the cultural whole which this has produced. That is why regional unrest cannot mean separatist tendencies, which would reduce India to a fragmentation of independent States. There is only one movement which aims at secession and that is the Dravidian movement, represented by Dravida Kazhagam (and even that is split on a matter of tactics). Clear out the Brahmans, to hell with the heroes of Hinduism and Sanskrit writings: 'What does the Tamil country need to develop?' asked Annadorei, one of the members of the Munnetra Dravida Kazhagam, in the course of the election campaign which won him a seat in the Madras Legislative Assembly. 'Gold? There's plenty up there on the roof of the temple (of Trichinopoly). What's stopping you from taking it?'

What stops the Tamils I cannot say, but the roof of the Rock Temple is as resplendent as ever and even the Dravida Kazhagam has refrained from touching it. The Union Government has tried to replace English by Hindi as the official language. To make a choice in this matter is as inevitable as it is inevitably arbitrary; but Hindi is a language which derives from Sanskrit, the language in which Pan-Indian culture has expressed itself in the South as in the North through the ages. Does the South reject Hindi? Possibly, but it is not at all certain. In 1952 I would have said yes. But on my return to India, less than four years later, I could not help noticing that people who had never known English were beginning to speak some Hindi. Do they reject Hindi as the compulsory language in Madras University? Yes, but the students learn it by attending the courses for popularizing Hindi which are held practically everywhere, and these courses are followed by examinations recognized by the University.

For that matter, if the Tamils set about expelling the Brahmans, the representatives of Aryan culture, it would hardly represent a triumph of progress: they would be expelling people as Dravidian as themselves for the most part, and the remaining high castes would have to clear out too. Dravidastan, if it is not a myth, will have to find its place within the Indian Union; although it is difficult to see what good it would do, and very few people even in the South, can see any advantage.

Hindu-Indian

I am often irritated by people who confuse the two terms Indian and Hindu. Well, I shall confuse them and have already done so, for not only is Indian culture Hindu, but Indian consciousness is Hindu. The Indians generally prefer the term Hindu in reference to themselves; and when one mentions that India also includes Muslims, Christians and Parsis, they are not in the least put out. This expresses, no doubt, at one and the same time a way of getting back at the British, who used the terms 'Indian' and 'native' indiscriminately and with equal contempt, and the new national pride of the Indian. The separation of Pakistan made him aware that Hinduism connotes India, that this is what belongs to him by right. Christianity is merely an imported religion and one, moreover, of Western origin (most people forget that Christ was Asiatic, if only to be able to claim Him the more completely for their pantheon). The fact that the Malabar Coast was inhabited by Christians who came from Asia Minor from the earliest days of the Christian Church does not matter a jot. It is true that Christians allege that they feel ill at ease in their country of adoption (or supposed country of adoption: most of them are converted Brahmans); they and the Parsis are possibly the only foreigners who have had no influence on Indian culture: the absence of any reference, open or implied, to Christian doctrine in Sanskrit writings of the south-west coast is the more striking since Hindu philosophers ceaselessly debate the tenets of real or imaginary opponents in order to exhaust all the logical possibilities of a problem. Christian opinion is too foreign; it does not so much as enter their field of logic. Which, however, in no way prevents Christians in India from strongly resembling Hindus: the leaning towards syncretism is the same, and I have heard the grandson of a convert announce that he could not understand anyone not dying in the faith of his forefathers, which is again a Hindu attitude correlative with syncretism.

The Indian Constitution (Art. 15) lays down: 'The State shall not discriminate against any citizen on grounds of race, religion, caste, sex, place of birth or any one of these factors.'

Congress, and in particular Nehru, wanted a secular State (unlike Pakistan which calls itself a Muslim State and is governed in accordance with the Koran). This was the only way to accommodate all the citizens of India in the new independent Republic and at the same time to allow the Government to draw up All-Indian legislation in every sphere. The Constitution, however, explicitly undertakes to protect cattle for the economic stability of the country: it would probably have been wiser to do away with half the cattle until there is more pasturage for them. But that is a detail; it was necessary to satisfy the large orthodox section of the community, who are very touchy when it comes to cows.

More recently, again, there have been measures concerning missionaries coming to India: it is a fair fight even if, in this case, nationalism rather than secularism is involved. The missionary is a hangover of the imperialist epoch; it is only right that he should vanish from the scene (in which case, why not the planter, and a whole lot of others?). We may be sure that in this matter the official regulations are inspired solely by national interest, as this is understood by the Indians: Nehru would never enact an outright discriminatory law; his rooted liberalism would forbid it.

In the country as a whole, however, it is a little different: Christians are criticized for their conversion, missionaries for having converted them. The recent Niyogi report on missionary activities in Madhya Pradesh – whose findings, incidentally, have not been accepted by the Union Government – could well have been underwritten by the government of a People's Democracy, which comment is not intended as praise. It has been realized, rather late in the day, that large tribes in that non-Hindu State were partly converted to Christianity by missionaries of different persuasions, and that Hindus could as well have done this work of conversion. The result is that the missionaries are held

responsible for the autonomist movements which have cropped up in such tribes as the Nagas of Assam. In a country where false witness is commonly and easily bought, there is no point in attaching too much weight to those who gave evidence. The report states explicitly that Christians cannot be good Indian citizens. The Niyogi Commission was obviously composed of strict and intolerant Hindus. The same intolerance is shown in practice, as a matter of fact, by those who regard themselves as most emancipated from their beliefs and their caste customs.

It might have been supposed that at least this Hindu hatred

would be directed only to the Christians, those Western converts: for, to be quite frank, it must be owned that many Indian Christians have provoked this attitude in their fellow countrymen. I myself, as a European, have become aware, from confidences received, that they rather smugly cultivate the mentality of exiles in their own country. They feel themselves 'different' from Hindus ('God, I thank thee that I am not as other men . . .'); they declare that they feel more at home with me than with Hindus; and I was shocked to my depths when an Indian woman told me that she prayed every day for the return of the Europeans to the government of India! It's a good thing to know that not all prayers are answered. That, of course, was an extreme case, and the Christians are gradually learning, with some surprise, that they are brothers to the Hindu, that the Hindu is their neighbour.

In any case, one might have supposed that the recent conversion of Untouchables to Buddhism would have been better received. During the celebrations of the Buddha Jayanti (2,500th anniversary of the Buddha's *parinirvana)* Nehru never ceased extolling Buddha, 'India's greatest son.' The truth of the matter is that the Brahmans were rather scandalized by this: and what about Rama? And Gandhi? It did not please them at all that the greatest Indian should be a non-Hindu. Nevertheless, mistrust of Buddhism cannot be compared with the hostility aroused by Christianity. Buddhism, which saw the light of day in India, can hardly be accounted an alien religion, and in any case it has remained an Asiatic one, the religion of a great many of the Bandung peoples whose leader India wishes to be. The foreign Buddhists living in India, at Nalanda, the ancient Buddhist University which they are trying to revive, or at the Mahabodhi Society in Calcutta, entertained the highest hopes when, in recent years, India officially and voluntarily associated itself with the Buddhist countries of the Far East in their attempts at a Buddhist revival and subsequently received the Dalai Lama, head of the Tibetan Church; they even began to quarrel amongst themselves about whether India would be converted to the Buddhism of the South or to that of the 'Great Vehicle.' The sudden conversion of some hundreds of thousands of Untouchables, however, has pleased neither the one nor the other: it was not religious but purely social motives which urged the Untouchables to discard Hinduism. But this does not stop their Hindu compatriots crying treason – those high-caste Hindus who would never have received the Untouchables among them, never have treated them as members of their society. Echoes of this outcry against the new converts have even been heard in the Delhi Parliament, which is up in arms at the attitude towards them, but can do nothing about it. All it could do was to refuse the Buddhist – as it had already refused the Christian – Untouchables the right to avail themselves of laws enacted for the benefit of the 'Scheduled Castes' (the official designation for inferior castes who receive Government aid).

As for the Muslims, the 1947 Partition still weighs heavily upon those who remained in India. No one trusts them any longer; they cannot be true Indians (naturally: they are not Hindus). There is no denying that Great Britain was wonderfully successful in her policy of dividing the two great Indian communities; for it is difficult to understand why the Muslims who did not choose to go to Pakistan should be held responsible for the existence of that State. However, it has the effect of confirming the Indian in his conviction that India is for the Hindus.

And those are my credentials for speaking within the compass of this far too small book only of Hindu India, since it is this India which sets the tone.

The Home and the World

ONE DAY I HEARD A FRENCHMAN ask an Indian woman of Brahmanical caste how the people of her country could live in peace with one another, since every caste, every religious sect, observed different customs distinguishing them from, if not actually setting them against their neighbours. At first sight it is indeed a marvel, in our time – when all social distinctions are frowned upon, when all women, season by season, are supposed to wear dresses of uniform colour and style – to find a country where everything goes; when a Pathan walks about Madras, he will wear, as in West Pakistan, wide trousers gathered up between the legs and a coloured turban with a flowing end. A Brahman woman from the South will not dream of changing her habit of wearing a sari if she goes to live in the North. For that matter, she will no more change her language than her clothes, and her children will continue to speak Tamil. The regional differences being so definite, no one is surprised at anything, and India is one of the few countries in the world where nothing seems ridiculous – although the slightest anomaly excites unashamed attention. Westerners very soon learn that you can do anything you please. Amongst them are those who, on arrival in India, and no doubt encouraged by the tropical winter, begin sporting a Newgate fringe. In the streets of Madras or Bombay the most outlandish get-ups are worn, such as would never be seen under English skies, or even those of the United States. But as a matter of fact these sartorial eccentrics are making a mistake: certainly you can see pretty well everything in an Indian city, but not just anything. A Pathan is labelled Pathan; a Parsi could not be anything but a Parsi; the appearance of a Brahman from the Tamil country or the

Rajput is known to one and all. But the European who goes out to do his shopping in a big town in shorts with a naked torso belongs to no society. Western or Eastern, and the Indian knows it.

But regional differences are the very least of it: each caste, each religious sect is differentiated from another by its dress, its calendar – there are at least three days calling themselves the New Year which are celebrated – and its festivals. Thus, in the same village very often several castes live in juxtaposition – in juxtaposition and in hierarchies – which denotes a minimum of harmony and of common agreement.

But one might equally well approach the question in another way and ask a particular Brahman why he finds it necessary to forbid his house to and exclude from association all who do not belong to the same caste or, rather, to the same sub-caste; why there are people known as Untouchables (which word, incidentally, is exceedingly inaccurate: it should be 'Unapproachable'). This social diversity, in fact, does imply complete segregation and cannot but imply it. The Brahman observes caste taboos as a matter of religious and moral duty; he will marry a girl only from the same sub-caste as himself, will eat only with his caste equals and perform distinctive religious rites.

Dharma

Among Westerners, in whom, at any rate in theory, the idea of the equality of man has been inculcated, who claim to believe in charity even if they do not practise it, the first reaction to this idea of total segregation and a system of prohibitions to safeguard it, is one of indignation; our whole moral sense is outraged by such inhumanity. I do not deny the inhumanity; I have no intention, indeed, of justifying the social system of castes; but let us first at least try to understand.

I shall have occasion to repeat that for the Hindu the individual human being is not the centre of the universe; he has only his appointed place, like other beings, in the cosmic order of things, the Vedic *rita*, the classical *dharma*, and his whole duty consists of remaining in that place, in doing, if he is born a Brahman, what is necessary for a true

Brahman, or for a true Sudra if he is born a Sudra. * This is in particular the fundamental teaching of the *Bhagavad-Gita,* the gospel of the Hindu, one of the finest works in the religious literature of India. In it the god Krishna exhorts Arjuna to pursue the war without thinking of the brothers he will kill, since this is his *Ksatriya* duty. Arjuna can never please the Lord better than by accomplishing his caste duty *in a disinterested way.* This last phrase seems to mean – amongst other things – that one should hold fast to one's caste duty but not to the privileges which high caste confers.

What is more, to be born into this or that caste is no accident, but the result of past deeds. According to the Hindu idea, you cannot, in fact, separate your adherence to the caste system from a belief in reincarnation, in innumerable reincarnations, without beginning, although they may have an end. And this theory of *samsara,* of the cycle of rebirths, is not gratuitous; it is itself part of the world order; it is the temporal or diachronistic aspect of *Dharma,* whereas the caste system is its synchronistic aspect, to use the technical jargon. Every one of our deeds has its result over and above its immediate effect, in the merit or demerit which it accrues for us, and that merit is measured by the deed's conformity with cosmic order. Thus, if I fulfil my duty as a Brahman, I shall be reborn as a Brahman or even something better; if not, I may be reborn into a lower caste. I have used the first person here as though identifying myself with the Brahman: that is not purely by chance. I am writing these words in India, and, without wholly accepting the Hindu world outlook, I cannot escape the influence of the atmosphere. Here it seems perfectly natural, even logical, to believe that the individual living today is no more than a link in an infinite chain of rebirths, and that such rebirths are the corollary to human inequality. Kant postulated a

---

* Theoretically the hierarchy of castes is as follows: Brahmans or priestly caste; Ksatriyas, princes, heads of State, and warriors; Vaisyas, tradesmen and agriculturists; and finally Sudras who devote themselves to serving the three higher castes who are twice-born – *dvija* – by initiation. But certain menial tasks are reserved for Untouchables. In practice, these categories cover innumerable castes, representing a complicated hierarchy whose features may vary from village to village. Thus Gandhi was of the Banya caste, which is the Gujarati merchant caste (and thus Vaisya), but in the Tamil region the predominant merchant caste is that of the Chetti.

just God who vouchsafed the reward of the good and the punishment of the wicked in the hereafter since this retribution is not dispensed here below, as unhappy Job already noted. This postulation does not particularly startle us and we find fault with it rather for being too logical, too neatly adjusted to our paltry human understanding: reincarnation is the Hindu answer to the same problem. The Hindu, like Kant, has no wish to foster revolt against the human condition, or despair, those Western inventions of the 20th century. Unless otherwise convinced, the Hindu believes he is undergoing – forgive me (why does one always drag opinions into what one is merely trying to describe?) – *is* undergoing the experience of reincarnation. The selfsame Brahman woman who was questioned by the Frenchman, and who was brought up in a quite modern and very rationalist way, readily claims that she feels the accumulation of her former lives weighing upon her.

The individual means much less in the world order than his deeds; and that is why Buddhism, which does not accept the principle of transmigration – of the eternal soul reincarnated – can at the same time assert that we are indefinitely reborn so long as we have not attained to supreme Enlightenment. The deed is not only, or even in the main, a profane deed, for that matter. Or rather, every deed from this point of view is a religious one, since it is the way of participating in and contributing to the maintenance of the world order; if I purify myself after touching an unclean thing or person, it is not out of contempt but out of religious necessity. The most important category of deeds is that of religious rites which, at any rate amongst the high castes, is what has remained of ancient Vedic ritual: it is tempting to compare this sacrificial religion, which prescribes this or that *puja* * to obtain this or that result – and quite often an entirely profane result – with what one knows of the Roman Catholic religion.

It must be admitted that the deity plays only a small part, that he is there because naturally the *puja* must be offered to someone; what really counts is the act itself; but the

---

* The *puja* is an oblation to a deity – flowers, Indian saffron, etc. – which the priest dedicates before the holy image while reciting various Sanskrit formulas, which vary from temple to temple; the ceremony is most beautiful and impressive; in the half-light of the sanctuary, the priest slowly rotates a platter of flaming camphor.

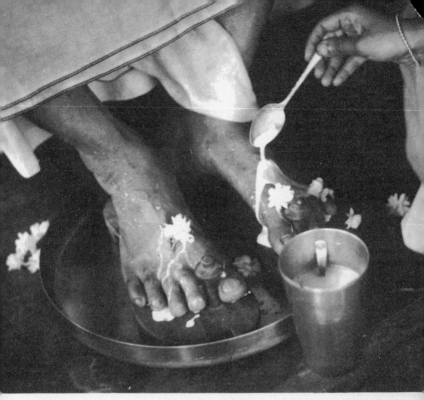

Pûjâ

value of that act is not apparent unless seenen in relation
to the world order; the sacrifice or *puja* is one of the most
genuinely free actions of the Hindu; and this because by
it he can influence his fate, that is, the cosmic order, insofar
as it affects himself.

There are also, as well as prohibitions, obligatory ceremonies and prayers for each caste. For a Brahman, the
burden of these obligations is so heavy that it is practically
impossible for him to fulfil them in the circumstances of
modern life; yet his status as a Brahman is bound up with
the discharge of these duties as much as with the prohibitions. So the Brahman of today who has become a town-
dweller in order to earn a living cannot avoid feeling deep
distress if he remains caste-conscious. I know a certain

The Home and the World

Pandit * in whom this distress is at its most acute. 'Am I still a Brahman?' he said to me one day. 'I travel with anyone, I teach non-Brahmans.' Indeed, I myself had been one of his pupils, and if tact prevented him from saying that he had even taught a *mleccha* (barbarian), I am quite sure he thought it. It was the greatest degradation for him; why should I have been offended? His profound religious feeling was inseparable from his membership of the Brahmanical caste. He was no longer sure that he had preserved the essence of what made him a Brahman, but he knew that he had been unable to avoid these breaches of the rules. Some days later I learnt that he was giving a lecture on 'The significance of the Vedas in modern life.' **

One important aspect of this theory of deeds and the world order is that everyone is responsible for his own fate: merit is not transferable and the act must be done by whoever wishes to reap its fruits. The *puja* in particular must be performed by the person who brings the offering. But, perhaps owing to the extraordinary refinements of ritualism, nobody, not even the Brahman, can be his own priest. There are specialized priests, Brahmans or others, who devote themselves either to service in the temples, or to *pujas* performed in the homes of those who send for them. The only way of ensuring that the merit of the *puja* shall revert to the individual seeking it is to pay the priest for the service rendered. The ritual fee is thus an integral part of the rite. I underline the point because the hurrying traveller will hardly ever come across any but this class of Brahmans in India: the priests who minister to the temples. And he will have a quite justifiably poor opinion of them. As in every country in the world, the lure of gain is very strong, and the ministering Brahman often turns into an arrogant and imperious beggar who thrusts his bowl under your nose and will not let you leave until you have, willy nilly, made sure that the merit of the *puja* reverts to you. For a Brahman to perform the *puja* for someone else is

---

* A Pandit, generally a Brahman, is one who has graduated not at a British type of university, but at a traditional Indian school. He is the real repository of Hindu culture.
** The Vedas are the earliest Indian writings, couched in archaic Sanskrit. They are collections of hymns which, together with the whole literature of exegesis and ritual accompanying them, constitute the charter of Hinduism in its oldest form, that of Brahmanism.

against the rules; in fact he thereby risks losing caste himself. Theoretically he is not supposed to be a temple priest for more than three years, but there are very few who give up so lucrative a position after that time, with the result that there are Brahman priests everywhere who constitute separate sub-castes and do not intermarry with other Brahmans. They are generally rather looked down upon, although no one knows how to dispense with their services. They are not to be confused with or taken as representative of Brahmans as a whole; they are invincibly ignorant, whereas the calling of a Brahman is to teach, and to teach without payment.

Lianas

Will the Hindu not revolt against a lot which classifies and labels him in the indefinite repetition of his reincarnations? The question is natural for us who always think that we ourselves are the measure of all things: my span of life is the span of my power; after my death, nothing exists, nothing happens – since I am no longer there. Not so for the Hindu, whose deeds endure whether he wishes it or not, without his consciousness, and will lead to his rebirth, somewhere or other on earth, in a given status for which he is held to be responsible. Our existentialists have never even dreamt of such an extension of human power; their recognition of total responsibility for all the happenings in the world seems to them quite agonizing enough. They would go out of their minds at the idea of a moral existence which has no other prospect than that of being perpetually re-created. But the Hindu feels no panic, no despair; his part in the cosmic order of things is a satisfaction and a relief. Far from opposing it, he learns very early in life that in coming into the world he has contracted three debts to be paid off during that lifetime: that to the Risis, the ancient seers who revealed the Vedas to the rest of mankind, to be paid by studying the sacred writings, which will perpetuate a knowledge of *dharma;* that to the gods, who help the universe to work smoothly, to be met by ritual sacrifices, by *pujas,* and specific prayers; and, finally, the forebears who gave him life are also owed their rewards, the only acceptable one being the continuation of their line; for their sake the Hindu must marry and beget sons. Chastity would be a great dereliction of duty; it would mean refusing to allow one's ancestors to be reborn. The wheel of *dharma,* that perfect symbol, can thus continue to revolve eternally.

We should be crushed by such a prospect; the Hindu is reassured by it. Yet he can hardly be called optimistic, as we shall see. If life held nothing but good, you could not wish to leave it. In fact, the final release is again seen in the continuation of an attitude of identification with the world order; one must submit oneself to it, let the universe cling closely about one. The idea of taking one's stand by making a stand would have no sense at all for the Hindu. What this means is that, in this country, man has not yet drawn a distinction between himself and the rest of the world, as he has done in our countries since the time of Socrates. That, too, is difficult to understand outside the atmosphere of India, which is itself inseparable from a relentless climate, or climates, and from hostile nature against which one can best contend by immersing oneself deeply in it. It needs a poet, a poet of cosmic unity, to be able to do justice to Indian landscape. What they have in common, I think, is their immenseness or rather the feeling that nothing here is on man's scale:

there are the enormous masses of the Himalayas, whose beauty is overwhelming rather than uplifting, so inimical does it seem to human effort; there is the luxuriance of flora and fauna in the jungles, where the marks of human labour are obliterated by the first rainfall; there is the hostility of the stark undulations of the Deccan Plateau, where one is astonished to find villages with emaciated herds of cattle grazing on a phantom pasturage; there are inexorable plains whose immensity seems to crush you. There are a few

◀ Jaipur Observatory   The river Jhelem in Kashmir ▼

exceptions, such as the Malabar Coast, where the gentle coconut palms blend with the velvet of the rice-fields – is it an accident that this was the cradle of Indian Communism which here, in relation to all else, appears as humanism? And in this enchanting landscape a far too large population, poverty-stricken and migratory, is on the go and must often be unaware of its good luck. Nowhere in India do the landscapes leave you unmoved, but each in its own

55

Jardin Zoologique d'Acclimatation
„Les Malabares"

way forces its beauty on you as a weight rather than offering itself to your view.

The fauna are less alarming, perhaps, because of their known and calculable dangers – serpents, panthers and tigers – than because of their teeming species and types. For a long time I personally, found the insects the most repulsive thing in India; every night they envelop you in a hostile and invisible web, in which mosquitoes very quickly come to seem positively genial, familiar as they are to the common run of people; you take refuge under a mosquito net to follow in safety the manoeuvres of fireflies, while enormous coleoptera (or are they something worse?) bang themselves against your frail fortress. Have teratologists ever been tempted to study those small quivering monsters perched on four paws bent at right angles till they form a cube, and whose heads, set on an exaggeratedly long neck, quiver at the slightest breath of air? And there are so many other kinds which one feels inclined to classify amongst nature's 'mistakes'. Surrounded by so much that is beyond him, in which he can recognize nothing that he understands, at the mercy of so much silent or avowed hostility, how should man not give up the struggle of resistance, of seeing himself as the centre and master of the world? Like the liana which clings to the tree and cannot live without it, the Indian becomes part of surrounding nature. He venerates the serpent which kills him no less than the cow whose milk nourishes him, thus refusing to separate the maternal and benevolent from the cruel and destructive aspects of the earth that bears him.

His divinities – and, above all, that Goddess who, from South to North, under different names, is everywhere the same – also have this dual aspect. One should remember that when one sees almost hysterical devotees fairly fling thenselves at Kali the Black, Kali the Cruel, with her red tongue hanging out, in the temple of Kalighat in Calcutta; she is offered flowers, coconuts and kids in propitiation; they know that she can be as kind as a mother, they adore her and they love her. At the southern tip of the Indian penin-sula the goddess Isakki, a replica of Kali, is at once the giver and devourer of children; her temples are filled with miniature cradles, votive offerings by women who want to become mothers; but if a child dies, that is also by the will of Isakki. Her legend is horrible and of unimaginable cruelty, but she is loved as much as she is feared.

Suddhi

It is possible that my rational British or American reader will not be satisfied with my explanation of caste: that every-one should have his duty, fair enough; that it should be a caste duty rather than a personal one, well and good. But does that make it necessary for them to judge their follows according to categories of clean and unclean? to forbid an Untouchable to approach nearer than thirty paces, for example? A Hindu would be wide-eyed with astonishment at such a question: as though one could set aside the 'diffe-rence' of uncleanness, as though, in this world, one could escape the interplay of clean and unclean! This gives a fresh insight into Hindu metaphysics, implicit as well as explicit: Hinduism, as I see it, differs from all the other great religions of the world in having a mythological basis. In its present-day form, it is the sum of contributions by disparate ele-ments, belonging to different layers of India's population, and whose fusion is now so complete, if not always harmo-nious, that to try and retrace its origins would be vain. At this point Hindus would protest that the divine heroes of Hinduism, such as Rama and Krishna, did have an historical existence. Possibly and even probably, but does anyone in his daily life turn to the teachings of Krishna the man, in the way that the Buddhist turns to those of Buddha? The Krishna in all his majesty of the *Bhagavad-Gita* has little or nothing in common with the shepherd Krishna and his youthful antics of the *Purana*.

The essence of the religion of Hindus in general consists of the observance of these rules of purity – *suddhi* – in which the moral and physical are indissolubly bound: if bathing in the Ganges at Banaras or in the lake of Puskar in Rajputana washes away my sins, that is because these consist essentially of bodily impurities in the first place. The fact is that the things that are considered unclean are to be found everywhere at the level of tribal society, and Indian society, though it has advanced far beyond the conditions of the tribe, has not been willing to lose the heritage of its tribal origins.

The unclean things are the same: a menstruating woman is unclean and whoever in the households touches her must immediately wash and change their clothes. For three days, she cannot take part in family prayers, and in the most orthodox families she remains unwashed and unkempt for

The Golden Temple of the Sikhs at Amritsar

three days in the outer room of the house, the room where guests are received and which is therefore not really part of the dwelling itself. A Hindu (and I mean very definitely a man, not a woman), who considered himself extremely emancipated, asked me once whether Christian women went to church when they had their period. I was obliged to say yes. My interlocutor, who was very well up in Christianity, said: 'But I take it they don't receive Communion?' I was almost ashamed to admit that they did, so conscious did I feel at that moment of his contempt for this *mleccha* religion. Of course I could have quoted Christ's words that nothing is unclean of itself. But how could he have believed me? How could blood not be unclean? It is largely for this reason that a good Brahman will wash his own clothes rather than give them to the laundryman, who washes linen defiled by blood.

The uncleanness of excrement is more comprehensible to us, but we could never attach to it the same importance that the Hindu does. In the first place the latrines, where they exist, are placed as far away as possible from the dwelling and, in accordance with the status of the family, have more or fewer holes. What is more – a miracle of training – as it is necessary to rid oneself at one stroke of all the pollutions of the night – that most inauspicious of all times – every Hindu has to start, and does start, his day by relieving himself; the whole of India relieves itself at the same time. And since most latrines are in fact the fields and roadsides, I strongly advise the traveller against walking about between 5 and 6.30 a.m. This performance, which lasts an extremely long time, is followed by washing, the second thing in the day compulsorily laid down for the Hindu. And this is all so little a matter of choice, so little profane, that the prayerbook composed by the monk Sivananda Sarasvati opens with the words: 'After having answered the call of nature, you take a bath.' So it is not surprising that the latrine-cleaner should be the lowest of all domestic Untouchables (for there is also a class of outcaste Untouchables).

The dead are of course highly unclean (although it is lucky to meet a funeral procession in the streets), from which arises the uncleanness of tambourine players *(parias)*, who escort the dead.

The barber, however, demonstrates the curious ambiguity

of holiness, repellent and attractive at the same time; in the South he is Untouchable, which is fairly easily explained by his calling. Hair and nails, those removable parts of the body, of the growth, of an individual, have always and everywhere been regarded as dangerous things. Those who are shaved or have their hair cut – for one cannot do without the services of a barber even in important ceremonies – must wash immediately afterwards. The custom still prevails in the Bombay district. But if you go farther North there is a complete reversal of outlook: the barber is the most important person in the village after the Brahman. Not only does he take part in all ceremonies, but he is al-

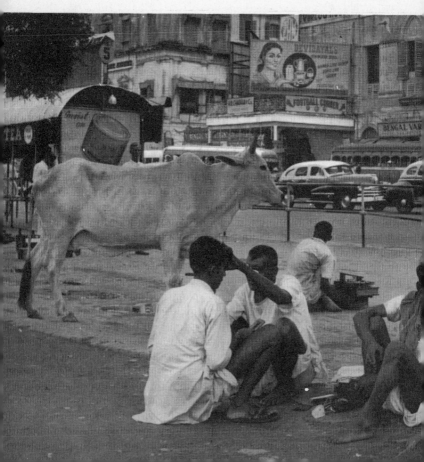

most the master of these ceremonies; he goes with the Brahman to invite prominent persons to attend weddings; he enters the houses of Brahmans and goes into parts where nobody else is allowed, sharing the secrets of the head of the house, to whom he often acts as counsellor. Some of his glory is reflected on his wife, who is also allowed into some houses; for is she not going to paint the women's feet red? On this score, she has the right of way everywhere, which accounts for her reputation as a go-between and procuress. She alone, apart from the gardener's wife – the one who delivers the flowers for the daily *puja* and for the women to put in their hair – has access to young girls of high caste and can induce them to leave their homes. She is shown in this role in more than one Bengali novel. In this case, then, the magic power of hair works in the barber's favour and confers genuine social prestige on him; his function makes him so sacred that for certain ceremonies he may be called upon to do the cooking, an honour generally devolving on the Brahman.

Tell me who you are

The uncleanness of a category of men is thus for the most part linked with the mythical uncleanness of objects which these men deal with in the practice of their profession. It is not the man who is disparaged, neither is it his occupation, which is socially indispensable, but the objects of his occupation.

This leads us to one of the primary meanings of the caste system: it is the form which the division of labour has taken in Hindu society. No doubt castes were exaggeratedly multiplied under the influence of various factors; the emergence of new techniques, or simply the juxtaposition of different techniques, is a good enough reason for separating several castes (and here I include in 'caste' a section of Untouchables, as they also form an entire hierarchy). There is a caste of potters who use a wheel and of potters without a wheel, of fishermen who go out to sea and cast their nets, and of those who fish only with nets from the shore, and of those, again, who fish by hand. The caste, based upon this idea of cleanness and uncleanness, was diversified, it seems, each time that an essential rule was found to have been contravened by one of its members. There are castes for the children of mixed marriages, and others for the children of bastards.

In every case the caste is integrated in a local hierarchy and plays its part in the exchange of those services which are fundamental the world over; there is, perhaps, in the last analysis, less distance, in fact or feeling, between ruling castes and servant castes than between the extremes of our social classes; the presence of the barber, even though Untouchable, at the great ceremonies in the life of the devout Hindu, and of a tambourine player at all funerals, are but two tokens of this amongst many, and these casual 'servants' are rewarded in kind at harvest time, receiving their share of delicacies or food when certain festivities take place. In their own way they are members of the village community and their function gives them an importance of which they are well aware.

There are, of course, other categories of Untouchables, or rather, in this case, of unapproachables: I shall cite only those breeders of black pigs in the north of Madras who reminded me irresistibly of La Bruyère's passage: 'One sees certain wild animals, males and females, all about the countryside, black, livid, and scorched by the sun, tied to the soil in which they root and grub with invincible stubbornness; they have something like articulate voices and when they rise to their feet, they show a human face; and, in fact, they are men.' These are not Louis XIV's peasants, but citizens enjoying the full rights of the Indian Republic. They live in conical huts made of borassus palm, where you have to crawl to get through the door and in whose interior you cannot stand upright. People are sitting all round it, practically naked, and not in the least interested in the car that has stopped on the road; the huts stand at some distance from the public highway, probably in order not to pollute it, and how could they have imagined that the car had stopped on their account? What dealings could they have with people other than their own kind? It was I who had asked to stop; I was being driven from Tirupattur, the stronghold of the strictest Vishnuism, to visit a palace in the neighbourhood. I must admit that the hovels made me forget the palace. I wanted to go closer; my fellow travellers, who were all *sudras,* refused to come with me, except for one who, as soon as we were alone, admitted that he was a Communist.

Yes, if it meant only this, the caste system would have to be destroyed, proclaimed an evil. But would it still survive so vigorously today if it were no more than this, than this savage segregation of a certain number of people whose only crime is that of rearing pigs for a living? In fact, for the majority, it is the sole means to social recognition: when a traveller arrives in a village, he states not only his name and that of his father, but also his caste and his village; then everyone knows where to place him and how to treat him. His position, however humble it may be, is his by right. He feels at home in it, and has a sense of his inherent human dignity, that of his caste. Here again, if we are to understand, we have to forget the sacred Western malady of individualism. The Indian individual has no existence other than within and through his caste; outside it he is lost, no longer a man but a social outcast, a nonentity.

You have to live here, under the Indian sun, to realise how much man means nothing in himself.. Family life is an illustration of the fact. It is probably true that the vast majority of Indian families live in one room, in enforced promiscuity, but it does not appear to distress them overmuch. And even amongst those who own large houses with an impressive maze of huge rooms, one is not a little surprised to find that no single member of the family seeks to be alone; the rooms stand empty – of furniture and people – except for the one where the entire family lives, receives its close friends, and sleeps. Fear plays a large part in this clinging together of the members of the family, but an undefined, nameless fear; the fear, quite simply, of being alone.

Nevertheless, even leaving aside the case of our pig-breeders, it must be acknowledged that the caste system does not exactly promote good human relations; the individual thinks of his neighbour in terms only of equality, inferiority, or superiority, and his attitude is deeply coloured by it. This is probably one of the reasons why the Brahman has become such an odious figure, he whom caste tradition calls upon to be disinterested and ready to give of the knowledge he possesses; he is seen simply as arrogant, harsh, and greedy for the money that will reinforce his social superiority. This is not entirely just, far from it, and I know many admirable Pandits who are a credit to their caste, and are poor because, apart from modern life and modern learning, they are completely detached from material things.

The Home and the World

But despite everything the system is more flexible than it appears; hierarchies are not absolutely immutable. There is the case of a certain low caste in Travancore, for example, which, by its unremitting work on the one hand and its imitation of higher castes on the other, has practically won for itself the third place in the society of that State. In the elevation of a caste there are always those two elements; one establishes one's economic position and becomes — I almost said more royalist than the king, but what I should say is more orthodox than the Brahman, in particular by adopting a vegetarian diet and by the strict exclusion of other castes, considered as inferior, from one's acquaintance.

But, it will be said, India is being modernized; caste is on its way out and one of the first measures of the Indian Government after independence was the abolition of untouchability. Amongst a section of particularly free-thinking city dwellers people claim to laugh at caste and its customs. In 1956 a large daily paper published a cartoon showing two Indians reading the paper and getting worked up about the 'castes' established by the Whites living in contact with the Blacks.

The fact is, Untouchability has been abolished on paper, and the result of this measure has been to eliminate the external signs of it. I came to India for the first time in 1950 and I have never seen, for example, water reserved for Muslims, a tap for people of caste and one for Untouchables in the stations. At least, there is nothing to indicate the distinction, but the upshot is that the orthodox Brahman never touches any water that he does not bring from home, or that is not of known origin. And one could cite many other instances of the strong survival of caste prohibitions; even in the stations, those of the South in particular, the counters where tea and coffee are served are manned solely by Brahmans, stripped to the waist and openly wearing the Brahmanical rope. The Government itself perpetuates the institution by making the Untouchables a separate electorate. Similarly, in every State, they enjoy advantages which set them apart from others: university and medical school places, etc., are reserved for students without caste; they are appointed by preference to certain administrative posts, and even as engineers and technicians. Paradoxically, with the system of places reserved for the least privileged section of the population, the Brahmans have to make do with what is left. Officially, and particularly in the South, where hostility towards them is reinforced by opposition to the Aryan culture that they represent, it has become the thing to despise the Brahmans. Indian culture as a whole will not benefit much by this, nor will the level of university studies; whether one likes it or not, the Brahmans have a tradition of culture, a taste for learning which makes these restrictions on their traditional activity very much to be deplored. These measures, in the long run, benefit only a negligible number of Untouchability. The Government has drawn special attention to it rather than let it sink into oblivion and it has not in any real sense relieved it of its economic inferiority. It is largely because they feel that everything is being done to maintain them in their outcaste status that recently the Harijan (the name Gandhi give them, meaning 'God's people'), taking the lead from their head, Dr. Ambedkar, were converted to Buddhism. In a less nationalistic age they would no doubt have been converted to Christianity. This is one of the most singular consequences of the Bandung spirit and the 2,500th anniversary of the Buddha's *nirvana*.

As for the Indian villages, which have remained unaffected by national currents, it can safely be said that the caste system, including Untouchability, remains unchanged. How many temples are still closed to Untouchables despite the law? And those which allow the Harijan to enter have introduced a new category of parias by forbidding the temple to non-Hindus, as witness the Tamil inscription hung at the gate of one of the most famous temples in the South: 'Admission to the temple is forbidden to Christians, Muslims and dogs . . .' Stricter still are many village temples, which allow only members of the local sub-caste of Brahmans to enter.

But what about Gandhi's campaigns for the Harijan in the thirties? It must be admitted that they remained a dead letter, and convinced only the converted, those who, like Nehru, had accepted certain Western ideas or who, in one way or another, felt extremely dubious about the value of the caste system. In any case the Mahatma sought above all to educate his Harijan, to raise them to the level of a fully human life. Little of this remains either, except for a few staunch Gandhiists.

It is no exaggeration to say that India's domestic policy,

at any rate at the level of the State Assemblies, is dominated by caste rivalries. The candidates standing for the various parties at elections are nominated from amongst the predominant castes in their constituencies. Even the Kerala Communists had to take this factor into account in the 1957 elections, although they refuse to admit that they systematically selected candidates in accordance with the caste of the voters. The Communist government, later removed by the Central Administration, represented the whole gamut of the most influential castes in the State – by chance or deliberate policy? Further: after the victory of the extreme Left I heard some Malabar Catholics declare that the failure of the Congress Party was owing to its nomination of non-Catholic candidates. This shows that caste rivalry combines to some extent with rivalry of religious 'communities', resulting in a checkerboard and an exceedingly complicated political game. From time to time Nehru appeals to the national spirit of his fellow countrymen, asking them to rise above their factional quarrels. The Prime Minister, one suspects, has no more effect than had the 'Father of the Nation', the Mahatma, whom the Indians now set up on their altars in order, no doubt, the better to forget his teachings.

On the very day that I write these words, I read in the *Times of India*: 'Measure to Abolish Untouchability: The Bombay Government is examining a proposition aimed at preventing persons who have been tried by the courts in connection with the law for the suppression of Untouchability from standing as candidates in elections to local government bodies (municipalities, etc.).'

Is it so very astonishing? I cannot see how the caste spirit could have been abolished by a stroke of the pen, nor yet by a propaganda campaign, insofar as it animates the whole of Indian life, including, and most particularly, religious life. Would Hinduism survive if caste disappeared? That is a question we shall have to look into later, but Hinduism as it is today is inseparable from caste society and the system of prohibitions which maintains it in its purity. So for caste to disappear there would have to be a complete remoulding, not only of society, but of Hindu mentality itself.

Well, there is some possibility today for that change of heart to occur; and let us say further that India will not

survive unless it does occur, if not at once, then at least gradually as economic life and all material circumstances are transformed. But of what country in the world is this not true? For whom, at the present time, is the ancient fabric of civilization, of outlook, not being shattered? The only difference is that India has a harder road to negotiate; she starts farther back and must reach the same stage as others.

The introduction of the railways already dealt a severe blow to the orthodox. For so mobile a population, which sets out on a journey so easily, a mechanical means of transport presented the greatest temptation; now, particularly, since economic necessity has scattered families far and wide, it is quite common to see parents taking the train to visit their children and the other way about, for there are occasions when the whole family must be together, when certain of its members must be there and nowhere else. But if you

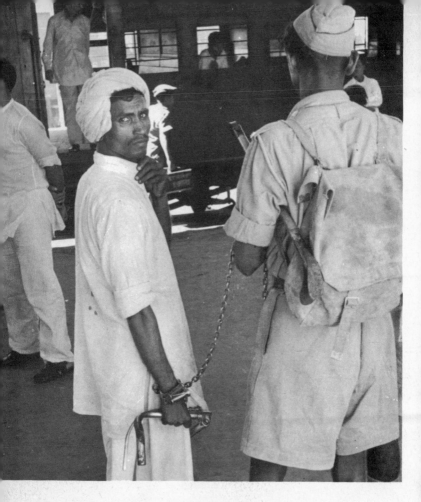

take a train or, nowadays, a bus, you are exposed to contact with other castes. And the odd thing is that, while the British were able to organize segregation — first-class on the railways being prohibited to Indians and the other classes prohibited to the British — the Indians have not even thought of separating castes in different compartments; they were left to their own devices too late in the day and habits had become too set, which shows that, to some extent, the circumstances of modern life can break down barriers.

But it is unquestionably the development of town life that will deal caste the death blow. How can you protect your Brahmanical purity when you go to work every day through the streets of a city rubbing shoulders with no matter whom? And what throngs there are in the Indian streets! The caste system is bound up with the village, where everybody knows everybody else and each is duly labelled. It cannot be transplanted as it stands into a vast urban centre, any more than can the patriarchal family whose standing it safeguards. The family group will be thinned out, for lack of enough living space in the towns, thus leading by easy stages towards the modern family of Western type. The question is whether the Hindu who is faithful to his religious beliefs will let go of what makes him a person of caste.

But there is a danger of understanding nothing of what will happen or of what is actually happening in India if

one does not take note of the fact that the most traditional Hindu society knows in certain circumstances – and has known for centuries – how to break through the barriers.

By fire and water

Though nature presents so many occasions for pollution, it also provides abundant means of purification which, incidentally, are to be found in every society which lives on its capital of myths: the endless interplay of clean and unclean, the eternal duality of the sacred, *tremendum et fascinans*.

Fire, the purest of the pure, is the object of worship under the triple form of the sun, the sacrificial flame, and the domestic hearth, which are mutually symbolic. A true Brahman cannot dispense with daily oblations to fire, which guarantee both the permanence of the cosmic order and the prosperity of his house. And no one will be surprised at the purifying power of the bright flame which consumes everything, from the human corpse to the clarified butter of the sacrifice. Even we, poor rationalists, who have lost contact with Mother Earth, dimly sense that to pass through fire is liberating. Not to mention that microbes cannot resist heat. No, what we feel is exactly what drives the devotee of Mariyammai, the goddess of smallpox but also the pre-eminent goddess, to walk over burning faggots every year after a prolonged fast, an experience of a complex religious nature, in which both the longing for purity and the desire for sacrifice go to make up a single passionate impulse. There is no worship without fire: the little lamp on the floor by the side of the altar, the great lamp suspended from a long chain, or with several wicks burning, the camphor flame which is slowly rotated before the divine image to consecrate the offerings, are so many examples of the power, in itself divine, of fire. That is also why it has the property of removing insurmountable barriers. A high-caste Hindu who would not under any pretext take food prepared by a cook of lower caste can accept raw rice from him, since ordeal by fire will serve to make it edible.

And if you are still sceptical about the 'sacredness' of fire, I would recommend you to go one evening – any evening – at the fleeting hour of sunset, to the banks of the Jamna in Mathura. Here a crowd is assembled before the temple,

between the river and an enormous oil lamp. This is the time of day when that other purest of the pure, the running water at our feet, is worshipped. As the flame shoots up, suddenly, high, lively, and blinding, one is deafened by the shout of the crowd, constantly repeated: '*Jamna ki jay!* Long live Jamna!' The river is worshipped, backs turned to the stream, while everyone strains towards the bewitching flame. They give themselves up to the enchantment of the dancing fire, they are drawn into the magic circle of the moving light. They even welcome the strain on the eyes, caused by the great frenzied fire, as inducing a state of torpor and sympathetic magic. It is sacrilege for anyone to recall the old man squatting by the hearth, who has gazed too long at the play of tongues of fire round the logs. The semi-ecstasy in which the crowd is now steeped draws you out of yourself, puts you in communion with the universe by effacing all consciousness of individuality. Slowly the flame dies down, they come to themselves, they rush to kindle at the sacred flame tiny earthen bowls, lined with oil, which they will float on the river on little mats of plaited sugar-cane. Those whose small vessels are carried by the current until the light is extinguished rejoice; water and fire have thereby united their beneficent powers. But there are many hazards: tortoises by the hundred may capsize raft and bowl with their huge backs, and cows, with no consideration for the sacred offering, catch at corners of the straw barques, jettisoning their cargo, and swallow them.

If the ceremony has failed to grip you, it is hopeless. If you have felt no surprise in seeing this throng, packed shoulder to shoulder, regardless of contact with unclean neighbours, you have missed the point. Fire wipes out all impurity; the castes come together in common worship wherein no distinctions can survive. And is it fire that achieves this miracle, or it is water? One may well ask.

The Jamna is not, indeed, the only sacred river in India; far from it. Water, too, is purifying and, by that token, is also to be worshipped. Is it not, moreover, one of the symbols of fecundity? There is not a trickle of water which has not its title to veneration and is not a source of purity. Each time I cross the Kaviri (the Ganges in the South) by train, I see one or two women in the compartment saluting it with the *anjali:* both hands joined vertically and slightly raised. The rivers are, indeed, so beautiful in this country,

The banks of the Tungabadra

reflecting the whole light of the marvellous sky, that one feels very much like adoring them, and Kaviri in the vicinity of Tiruchirapalli (Trichinopoly) would be the one I should choose above all. It flows between rice fields and curtains of coconut and borassus palms, and distant blue hills with exotic outlines. Its waters, often very shallow, take on all the colours of the sky in a region where sunsets are especially glorious. Its harmony and tranquillity are, once again, beyond the human scale, and it is not hard to believe that the impulse to pray rises involutarily in that ambience, as a tribute to an almost tangible transcendency. To plunge oneself into such a river is a benediction. But what am I saying? A stagnant pool has the same virtues; one bathes in it, one draws one's daily water from it. The complete divorce that we have made for generations now between the spiritual and the physical has to have taken place for us to feel disgust at the sight presented by the Banaras *ghats:* doubly sacred waters like those of the Ganges cannot be injurious to the body if they are good for the soul. One might bear in mind the bathing-pool at Lourdes, which, laden with the germs of the sick, retains for the pilgrims its miraculous properties. The Hindu who washes out his mouth with water from the Ganges is in no way put off by the proximity of someone else who is putting his body to rights. The marvel lies for him in the fact that this neighbour cannot sully him whilst he is in the water, even if he is of lower caste.

Too much impurity divides; total purity unites. The unbelievable crowds of Indian pilgrimages are the antidote to the crumbling of Hindu society. At these great concourses each year the press of people is so tremendous that they

leave behind dead and injured; suffocated, trampled on, these will never return to their homes, but the pilgrimage, the sacred bath have washed away their sins, lifted the weight of evil deeds from the lives that are to come. The multitude is at its greatest at Kumbh Mela, a combined pilgrimage and fair, which is held every twelve years at a different temple. But there is an almost constant stream of pilgrims to Haridvar, Prayag (Allahabad), and Banaras (Benares) on the Ganges, to Rameswaram and Madura in the South, to Pandharpur and Nasik in Maharastra, and to Puri in Orissa, to mention only the most famous of the places which catalyse and dispense holiness.

The tourist, having cursed the crowd for bringing his car or his ricksha to a standstill, is more than a little staggered to find on reaching the bank of the river or sacred lake at the bathing hour – in the early morning or late afternoon – that there are almost as many people in the water as out of it. They are all at various stages of their ablutions, sprinkling themselves with the traditional copper *lota*, spitting, puffing, drinking, plunging their heads under water, regardless of the nameless throng pressing round them; women mingling with men, the thin material of their saris plastered to the skin in a startling way. But indecency is a matter of convention and who could think evil in these most holy places? (It should be said that our bathing-suits appear very improper to Indian eyes.)

And this seems a good opportunity to say, in passing, that the separation of the sexes is a very definite feature of Hindu society. Women go out very little as a rule, and the higher the caste the more seldom. Though they exercise more authority in the home than is generally supposed, they are very rarely seen by their husbands' or fathers' friends. They never speak to a man unless it is absolutely necessary, and a well-brought-up man will not address them. It may be worth noting how this affects the Western woman who asks questions and talks openly. The Indians will show her every mark of respect, but she should beware of chattering too freely; they would pretty quickly assume that they could take any liberty.

If, for once a woman does go out with her husband, she has to walk respectfully behind him (though I am not saying that all of them do so nowadays). When they travel, women are engulfed in the 'ladies' compartment' with babies and bagage – oh, the unbelievable array of family luggage of every shape and size! – while husbands and fathers sit in state in the 'general compartment'. When the train stops for meals they ask you civilly – or not so civilly – to give up your seat so that the lord and master may take his place on the bench and be served with the rice or *chapati* secreted in one of the innumerable bags stacked in the corner. I must admit I know nothing more frightful – or more picturesque – than the women's compartments on Indian trains. Women's inferiority is outwardly reflected in modes of speech too; the husband addresses his wife in the second person singular, whereas she uses the formal term, never utters his name, and refers to him as the father of her children. In public it is always the husband who makes the decisions, gives the orders, and sits down while his wife remains standing. Our feminists, I have no doubt, feel a burning anger rise. But let me reassure them: in the privacy of the home the woman reassserts her full rights; expressions of love between married couples are as fond as anywhere else in the world. The man knows how to show tenderness and readily listens to his wife's advice. That's all very well, you will say, but how can there be love in a society where marriages are arranged by the families and according to astrological and economic calculations? All the young women I was able to question on this delicate matter looked at me with shocked expressions. 'Love? But that comes after marriage.' The reply was the more convincing in that it was made, in most cases, by young women who had married relatively late, had a profession, and who to my knowledge had dreaded the marriage forced on them by the family. In the uniting of hearts physical attraction no doubt plays a large part, but not alone for long. The husband and wife acknowledge and accept each other as engaged couples do in our countries.

The apparent inequality of status for men and women may have arisen as a means of protecting the weaker sex, more coveted and more vulnerable among this hot-blooded people perhaps than anywhere else. The Muslim invasions were largely responsible for the present state of affairs; the imperial and royal harems, always being replenished, inculcated fear of strangers, of the man who approached you in the street or at your house; if he showed an interest in you, he probably had designs on your wife. But imitation

Wedding in Calcutta

of the conquerors has undoubtedly also led a great many
Hindus to veil their women, for whom seclusion became
a sign of aristocracy. One still sees some Hindu ladies going
about in *pardah*, in a car with drawn curtains or the end
of a sari held across the face. Only Muslims, however,
affect the heavy black or white *bourqah* with netting up to
the eyes which, under tropical skies, must be real torture.

That the Indian woman is in fact greatly respected and
deferred to is shown by the religious part she plays in
relation to her husband. She joins him in his prayers and
his offerings, which have no value without her presence;
and this has always been so. It is she, with her maternal
function, who symbolizes the everlasting joy of cosmic
fecundity: the deity very easily assumes a feminine guise,
more accessible than the immutable Absolute. There are
sadhus and *gurus* of both sexes. So there is really nothing

to be surprised at in the fact that woman's true status is revealed in public precisely in places where contact with the other sex, the glances of the other sex, could never be unchaste. Thus she mingles in the crowd more freely than we should be able to do in the extreme promiscuity of the sacred bath.

The Home and the World

The scene presented at its most exaggerated by the pilgrimage and that at the temple pools is enacted daily wherever the poor take their bath. Those who have none but public water for their use go to the nearest stream or pond; bathing and doing their washing are performed as a rite in a literally religious silence. The body and the clothes are washed at the same time, often without soap. There a man, here a woman, is beating some part of his clothing on the stones of the bank. The woman wraps herself round in one end of her sari while she washes the other. Her muscles stand out under the wet material. The man is wearing nothing but a rag between his legs. Not a joke, not so much as an exchange of remarks. Each is absorbed in the task, and if you draw close, you hear one or other murmuring prayers. Only the children enjoy the fun of the bath.

In point of fact, the reconciliation by water of the divided

had in the past, and still has in many villages, an important reservation: Untouchables are too unclean to become touchable in water. In the fight between pure and impure, it is the water that comes off worst here. By contact with the Untouchable water is polluted for a man of caste; it is no longer clean except for extreme uncleanness. Nevertheless, when one considers the barriers erceted by caste, it is impossible to forget the extraordinary phenomenon of the crowds united by a desire for purification and salvation.

It is not, indeed, wholly desirable that these apparently insurmountable walls, which fall of their own accord in certain well-defined circumstances, should disappear too rapidly under the pressures of profane modern life. Already too many Indians on their return from studying abroad repudiate their family and caste traditions – which, after all, form the whole of their unique framework of ethics – but put nothing in their place. So many of them have become virtual robots whose only god is that of material progress, who pay tribute to America as the land of television and refrigerators and have learnt nothing else from it. Dare I use a much discredited word which nevertheless seems unavoidable here: if the caste system disappears too rapidly it will mean the death of the Indian soul.

Which takes us to the threshold of India's crucial problems today: the problems of economic life.

Daily Rice

THE WEST HAS ONLY JUST AWAKENED to the poverty of one-half of the globe, and to that of India in particular. It is quite likely that even Britain herself is still amazed at what is being revealed today about her former colony. While in India I had occasion to read copies of English papers of a century ago, where I found, for example, a long article describing, in enormous detail and with exclamations of compassion, the overflowing of the Rhone. There was less, as you might expect, about the inundations which, year after year, ravage whole areas of India, destroying harvests and breeding famine and disease. Yet the 19th century, like every other, was full of such catastrophes. In the time of the mughals and even of the Delhi Sultans, Muslim chronicles record innumerable famines. They seem to have increased at the beginning of the 20th century, and to this day the problem of food comes to the forefront with the end of the dry season each year. During the last World War the people of many occupied countries in Europe learnt what it is to worry about the lean time between two harvests, though they are fast forgetting it. Here in India that worry can never be forgotten. Some years it may be less grave than others, but it is ever present, the theme of down-to-earth political debate and the source of hardships for India's 'teeming millions'. There are, indeed, some for whom the lean season lasts six months or more, in good years and in bad, and this throughout their entire lives. This frantic poverty, which will not let you rest, becomes

an obsession once you have seen it at close range; you
begin to understand a little why so many of the more privileged prefer not to know of it; otherwise they could never
go on sleeping in peace.

Here are some figures: at the time of the 1951 census
the population was 356,879, 394 (and probably more; it is
thought that a significant percentage, 11 per 1000, was
overlooked by the census clerks), in an area of 1,177,000
square miles, or two and a quarter acres per person, but
only 0.84 acres of cultivated land; that is, well under an acre
a head in a country 82.7 per cent of whose inhabitants live
by agriculture. The figure of the average annual income
per head varies; it was estimated at 262 rupees in 1954–55
(that is, just over £ 19 or $ 50), and the immense fortunes
of the privileged few are naturally included in this average,
which is, moreover, an official figure. It is lower than it
was in the thirties, but shows a slight increase over that
for the period 1948–50, immediately following independence.
There is no question at all but that misery has grown during

the past two centuries, as is shown by the curve of famines. The Indian population is growing with disquieting rapidity, and is increasing still further with the slight advances in hygiene and the fight against infant mortality. The annual birth rate in the years 1941–50 was 40 per 1000, while the death rate was not above 27 per 1000; which represents an absolute annual increase in the population of four and a half million. At the time when Europe was being industrialized to increase the volume of employment and of the means of subsistence, the Bengal weavers who might have meant competition to the English cotton masters were crippled, and all measures were taken to destroy Indian industry in embryo. To this must be added, even today, the lack of rapid communications, so that a region enjoying plenty is in practice unable to relieve another in a state of famine.

Of course, in fairness to those who developed the land, one must also emphasize the inexorability of the tropical climate which leaves the absolutely essential harvest, year after year, at the mercy of too much or too little rain. Between 1948 and 1952 the monsoon in the South was so inadequate that a state of scarcity became endemic. The 1951 *Census Report,* giving the rain belts of India, makes this comment, which would sound laughable if it were not for the tragic implications: 'In these zones (where less than 15 to 30 inches of rain falls a year), seasonal fluctuations are so common that they are more or less regularly expected.'

Regular fluctuations: there is a problem to stir the imagination of any government concerned for the well-being of its people; irrigation schemes must be one of its primary preoccupations.

But, irrigation or no irrigation, the agrarian situation is yet another bad debt bequeathed by the British. In the areas which were formerly what was called British India, as distinct from the nominally independent princely States, the practice of farming out taxes led to the development of great landed estates, badly managed, badly farmed, and worked by hungry peasants who were little better than serfs. Thus another problem facing the independent Government of India is that of land reform which, in view of the variety of regional conditions, also involves the State governments.

Naturally the extreme poverty is accompanied by illiteracy in a country where, until recently, there has been practically no free primary schooling, though primary Education Acts were passed in a number of provinces during 1918–20, following the 1919 Government of India Act. It is an understatement to say that the vast majority of Indians are unlettered. They lack the fundamental education necessary for the most everyday matters, which explains the attempt at a 'basic national education' launched under Gandhi's auspices in the late thirties. The rudiments of hygiene are unknown, and it makes one shudder to see a mother offer her child a titbit grey with dust, for which he contends with the flies. A street vendor goes by selling ices, not our luscious ices, but small pieces of solidified water coloured with completely synthetic fruit juice. It is hot. The indulgent mother gives her baby the ice to suck. A hundred and one street scenes of this kind make one shudder.

The peasant who cannot afford to buy fertilizer could at least use what he has to improve his land; but he uses cow dung for fuel, not fertilizer; he persistently grows the same crop on the same plot of land, and so on. But what can be said or done when one is dealing with people stultified by age-long undernourishment and when these people constitute practically half the total population? Here more than anywhere else in the world you realize that a certain material level is essential to human development, and the majority is still well below that level. Only a slow, vegetative existence is possible for them.

There are so many nationalist parties who waged the fight for independence with the aim of taking power, without bothering overmuch about the welfare of the nation, that Nehru's government deserves unqualified admiration and praise for the courage with which it has tackled these tremendous problems. India disseminates its propaganda abroad pretty well, and the whole world is aware of the novelty of the Indian solution: a skilful harnessing of opposites, or possibly of contradictions; liberalism and state control harmoniously combined to lead the country to prosperity. Private capital, threatened from the outset of independence, has been given safeguards, for there is no way of doing without its investments. Not so long ago the rich Parsi Birla was received by the Communist Prime Minister of Kerala, which was short of investment capital. The key industries are being progressively nationalized; the engineering industry is owned by private or government undertakings.

But obviously it is the Five Year Plans which command the most attention. Since 1956 India has embarked on the Second Five Year Plan, on a larger scale and more ambitious than the first. It intends to direct and control production and investment in every sector, and to let private capital participate in developments directed from above. It is setting up, financing, creating, steering, dealing with everything, altering everything, but destroying nothing. It is a typically Indian approach, of course, in that it does not seek to break up anything, trying to utilize every existing source of wealth, and in that it does not seek to use compulsion or impose anything by force. It constantly harks back to Gandhi and to his doctrine of non-violence, of which, however, very little remains in the actual conduct of Government. No one will compel the manufacturers to give what they have, no undue pressure will be exercised to make them invest their capital to advantage. But, on the other hand, how often reports appear in the papers describing clashes between the police and crowds of demonstrators, whether workers on strike or Gujaratis who refuse to resign themselves to the loss of Bombay; *lathis* crack – those ironbound sticks used by the British police, so often decried by Congress members then in gaol – and shots are fired, only too often leaving dead and wounded on the scene. What amounts to a small war is being waged in Assam, against the Nagas, a 'terrorist' tribe, passionately autonomous, and deaf to the voice of Mother India. But police and army measures are not included in the Plan. So it comes to this: that the fundamental inspiration is not so much a distinctively Indian product, as is fondly proclaimed, but has sprung fully armed from Nehru's own heart and mind. Schooled in European socialist ideas, but opposed, by his aristocratic temperament, to totalitarian methods, he is trying to reconcile the irreconcilable, or what at least appears to be so today: to combine social and political freedom with economic control, wealth for the few with the wellbeing of all. That dream is so noble that instinctively one hopes he will prove to be right, and will succeed. It is as though in his own person he were the New Left in power, an intellectual who is not above technical details, a Utopian and a realist. How can he help envisaging the reconciling of contradictions, since he carries them within himself?

The paradox of this humanist policy is that it is meant to apply to a country where the individual is still so little aware of his freedom, where man has still to discover across the barriers of caste, that men are brothers, where the brotherhood of man seems an ideal even more remote than in our countries, which is saying a good deal. By employing 'democratic' methods – a word very dear to the Indian Prime Minister – it appears that Nehru is trying to hasten for his compatriots the discovery of the value of human dignity, and in his desire to educate his people there is something very moving and at the same time tragic, he is almost alone in desiring it and he knows it. He preaches in and out of season; he knows both the joy of being listened to by the wide public that flocks to his lectures and the bitterness of seeing his words remain a dead letter. But though his ideas, being what they are, cannot be adopted by those unable to understand them, he has the hope, at least – through the Five Year Plans – of setting the nation to work. When he opens a plant he offers food to the workers who, having eaten their fill, will be more able to take in what he says.

Gateway of the Palace of the Maharajah of Baro

Unreal obstables

Thus here is an India, the greater part of whose population still lives by its primitive myths, imprisoned within its intangible laws of the clean and the unclean, jumping in one go to the last stage of social evolution in the 20th century, the stage of a planned society, and this under a regime that sets itself the aim of being democratic. Will it work? Is it not quite Utopian? The sceptics will ask: how can a people caught up in age-old customs adapt themselves all of a sudden to the demands of productivity and planning; will they abandon the ancestral wooden plough and potter's wheel to work machines? This raises a preliminary question which should be examined. I strongly suspect that behind these misgivings lurks the stale smell of racial prejudice which is unwilling to disclose itself. But let us rather examine the objections; there is a great deal at stake.

First of all there is the pitying look which the strong, free man casts on the 'poor Indian,' the prisoner of his religious views. The caste system, the belief in reincarnation, and in the law of retribution according to deserts, are thought to be particularly pernicious because they rule out any attempt at progress. That is the greatest if not the latest nonsense trotted out by anti-clericalism; it seizes on concepts and turns them into human attitudes, as if life were not always infinitely more complex and, above all, more dynamic.

Of course the Hindu scriptures are totally incompatible with modern life, and even with any kind of regular working life, amongst the high castes, the religious observances of the master and the mistress of the house are so time-filling that it is hardly possible for them to go out: prayers at the three great moments of the day – sunrise, noon, and dusk – which ensure the orderly progress of the days, the unpropitious times when it is forbidden to undertake anything whatsoever, and the various prohibitions inside and outside the home, make any participation in modern social life out of the question. There is the case of the Nambudiri Brahmans of Kerala, for whom everything – marriage customs, laws governing inheritance, unequal status of the eldest and the younger sons – aims at keeping the eldest son, the head of the family and owner of the patrimony, tied to the house where he is supposed to carry out rites and observe all prescribed laws. In any case, they generally live in the country and are landed proprietors. Landed proprietors, and thus also relieved of the necessity to earn a living, are the devout village Brahmans who still observe their caste *dharma* as best they can. And, naturally, there are also reactionaries who prefer to live in the past and believe that the knowledge of previous centuries is infallible, as witness this interchange heard in the Union House of the People between Nehru and Members of Parliament on the subject of the law of Hindu succession (which aimed at giving rights to women): 'In a world of rapid changes, said Mr. Nehru' (I quote from the *Times of India* of May 9th, 1956), 'nothing seemed to him more misplaced and ridiculous than to go on thinking as though one were living a thousand or two thousand years ago. What was the population of India two thousand years ago? It has been estimated that it was infinitely smaller than today.

'*Mr. N. L. Sharma*: 56 *crores* (560 million) 5000 years ago.

Mr. Nehru: That is the voice of experience speaking.

Mr. Sharma: The experience of *sastra.* *

Mr. Nehru: I regret to say that I do not accept this statement of the *sastras,* if any of them ever made it.

Mr. V. G. Deshpande: What guaranteed authority has the Prime Minister for the figures he cites?

Mr. Nehru: If Mr. Deshpande or the other Member wants an authority I suggest he attends an elementary science course . . . My humble effort was aimed at this: to show this House that it has become important and vital for us, if we want to survive as a nation and still more if we want to make progress, to drop the way of thinking of our friend opposite, for this way of thinking is very interesting but is only fit for an ethnological museum.'

But are the reactionaries a prerogative of India? Everything I have seen in other places tends to show that, once again, as so often in the course of his history, the Hindu is adapting himself, assimilating what has become vitally necessary to assimilate, without repudiating the past, but also without adhering too rigidly to that past. There are, as a matter of fact, even in Parliament, less progressive voices than that of the Prime Minister which are concerned

---

* All the ancient treatises on the most diverse subjects, religious and secular, were called *sastra.* All of them are regarded as sacred.

to point out the continuity between past and future. Has it not been said that today's Parliament replaces the *risi,* the original mythical seers?

Caste survives, we said, in all its strictness. Quite true; but already it co-exists with its own grave-diggers. How many Brahmans at the present time have their sons educated according to strict Brahmanical laws, by placing them under a tutor who will instruct them in the Vedas? How many allow them to be taught traditional Sanskrit studies? At Kaladi, the presumed country of the philosopher Sankara and one of the strongholds of Brahmanical orthodoxy, I was greatly surprised to learn that the parents of the pupils at the Vedic school received a relatively large sum each month in return for which they agreed to send their children to a master who would teach them to recite the Veda. It is not an isolated case; in fact the problem of the daily rice is too serious for any Indian who does not have a large enough patrimony. He knows that his son must have a trade and earn his living while remaining a good Hindu, which is rather like squaring the circle. What can a Brahman priest, learned in the Vedas, earn compared with someone who has consented to study modern subjects and becomes an engineer? And one sees how, bit by bit, even in the countryside, the prestige of money catches up with that of caste before supplanting it; those who come back from the towns with more money than their parents ever had command the respect of one and all. It was at Kaladi, however, that I was expelled from the main village street and from the approaches to the Vedic school; the street was entirely reserved for the local sub-caste of Brahmans and the sacred sounds issuing from the Vedic school where the children were reciting were too holy for my *mleccha* ears.

In the streets of Tirapattur I have seen adolescent Brahmans whose haggard faces bore eloquent witness to their lack of sleep; most of them go every morning, between the hours of 4 and 6, to a master to learn the Vedas, while during the day they attend school like everyone else. And orthodoxy repels many young people more than it attracts them. Or else, as in Kerala, the general atmosphere is emancipated enough for the young men of high caste to break away from all traditional ties: the Communist Party in Kerala was mainly recruited from amongst the Nambudiri Brahmans and the Nayyars, two castes renowned for their

orthodoxy; the later removed head of the Communist Cabinet is a Nambudiri. Or again, and this is the situation in Tirupattur and in part of the State of Andhra, another centre of Indian Communism, the atmosphere is too orthodox for young Brahmans to rebel against it, but the Communist Party recruits amongst young people of lower castes reacting against the exclusiveness of the Brahmans, who, for their part, did not seek it: during the Second World War they wanted Sanskrit classes to be opened to non-Brahmans at the University of Tirupattur, and this move caused a strike amongst University teachers.

In the conflict between orthodoxy and the demands of modern life, though it has barely begun, it is already clear which will be defeated. The main factor slowing down the evolution now in progress – here as everywhere else – is the women, who, I have seen with my own eyes, pester their husbands not to contravene the rules of their caste. But they, too, want to eat and to feed their children; and once they consent to come out of their homes and see what is going on outside, they prove to be as adaptable as the men. Though the mothers may be illiterate, the daughters are so no longer; plenty of them are even at the universities.

The present evolution entails for members of high castes that, in gentral, they take up professions traditionally forbidden them. Thus a Brahman is not allowed to cultivate the soil himself or be employed by anyone to do administrative work. Yet already in 1901 the Bombay Census showed that 47 per cent of Brahmans were engaged in administration and agriculture. It even appears likely that the Brahmans will have to compromise, and are compromising, faster than anyone else, since the prohibitions affecting them are more far-reaching.

Changes will be speeded up by the fact that caste and social class hardly overlap at all, and will do so less and less. The time when Brahmans were assured of a living no matter what happened is past; the rajahs prided themselves particularly on caring for poor Brahmans, but the Indian Republic has deprived them of the means of this liberality. At the same time – and also for economic reasons – their services as tutors and priests are less and less in demand. Things are at the point where, even though beliefs remain intact and the prohibitions still in force, the situation slowly changes to the detriment of the orthodox castes; traditions are preserved as best they can be, not everything is jettisoned, but one's got to live. A Brahman who has to become a factory worker – this situation was beginning to be reflected in the 1921 Bengal Census – may still retain his Brahman consciousness; but one can well believe that he learns something about simple human brotherhood. It is possible that, in the first stages, the high castes withdraw themselves behind rigid outward orthodoxy, aware that, where essentials are concerned, the game is up. But the following generation is bound to go further. For these aristocrats, however, there are new openings which are not too repellent once they know of their existence: the liberal professions are practically their exclusive domain. I do not know whether there are any statistics on this, but certainly a high proportion of doctors, lawyers and engineers are Brahmans of Ksatriyas. In point of fact, it is doubtful whether it is the Brahmans who, taken all round, are putting up the greatest resistance to economic pressure; it may be that, because they have an intellectual tradition, the breach in their universe goes deeper straight away and entirely transforms their way of thought.

The rigidity is perhaps greater amongst those castes who,

for centuries, have striven to win recognition of their high rank and have not quite succeeded, such as the Nayars of Kerala or the Maharashtrians of the State of Bombay.

As for the lower castes, they submit much more easily to the requirements of the day, money having gained for them the prestige which the traditional social hierarchy does not provide.

Of course, so long as caste-consciousness survives, upheld and reinforced by family ties, people are reluctant to move from one area to another or to leave their village for the neighbouring town. But this does not present a real obstacle, for, from top to bottom of the social scale, things work out the same way; a man will leave his native village or small town for the big city which offers him employment, but he comes back to find a wife in the place where he was born; his wife goes back for her confinements; he rushes there whenever a member of the family falls ill. The big factories in the Bombay district and in the northern plains thus record great seasonal movements amongst their workers. A considerable proportion of them – as high as 40 per cent, it is said – come from more or less distant villages and return there at fixed times of the year. The peak periods of absenteeism are the same everywhere; at harvest time, when the factory worker reverts to agricultural labour on his own or another's family plot of land, for the hard work of harvesting is well paid; and at the time of weddings – certain months of the year, particularly the end of the winter and the spring, are especially favourable, and some fine day the young worker will vanish from the factory in response to a family summons; the ideal wife has been found for him – I almost said the ideal daughter-in-law for his mother. Often, indeed, he leaves his bride in the village, with his parents, and regularly sends her money from the town. In the factory he has no caste, no tradition, and, to all intents and purposes, no beliefs. No sooner does he return to the fold than he reverts to his ancestral customs and adapts himself to them without a murmur.

Another thing that is very commonly said is that the taboos on food entail criminal wastefulness in a hungry country. The British increased this wastefulness by their mere presence as *mleccha*. The innumerable dishes which came to their tables and were removed to the kitchen, barely touched, were thrown to the crows, it is claimed. It is quite likely, and there must have been incidents of the kind. But I must say that taboos hardly exist today for empty stomachs. Over a period of two years I saw my half-filled breakfast plate regularly cleared. The servant, of Nayyar caste, stayed for a minute or two in the room where the meal had been served and must have gobbled up my leavings with extraordinary speed, probably so that I should not observe her sin. She had six children and an unemployed husband and earned 40 rupees a month (roughly £ 3 or

As for belief in reincarnation, it is no doubt one solution to the social problem; there is no need for me to trouble myself about the pitiable fate of my neighbour; he has brought it on himself. But belief in reincarnation does not hinder anyone from working for his own social advancement, from increasing his patrimony or his knowledge. On the contrary, it is an incentive for everyone to do better. Of course, it is far from being a question of working for the good of others, and one does indeed come across a total ignorance of other people's misery amongst the privileged; a rich Parsi lady refused to allow her car to take me through the working-class quarters – one might say the shanty town – of Bombay. She had never been there herself because 'it wasn't done.' A Hindu lady in the South assured me that the people in a certain village – which she had never seen and where I had been very frequently – had a meal of fish and rice every evening 'like everybody else.' In point of fact this village was one of those where the lean time between harvests lasted six months, and I could not help knowing that during those months they did not have a proper meal as often as once in two days.

All right. But our Western societies, though they may have gone in for charitable works, were not based upon charity; what, for example, would the working class of our industrialized countries have ever got if they themselves had not revolted? In any case in India there is a theory of giving or, more precisely, an idea of exchange, which may help very much towards the functioning of a modern society. At no level does the Indian accept the idea of a free gift. If he gives alms to a beggar, it confers social prestige on him and humbles the beggar, and that is his reward; if he gives food or clothing to a *sadhu* – one of the innumerable hermits whom India still venerates and cherishes today,

Daily Rice

as we shall see – he thereby acquires a kind of pledge of salvation, or at least merit whose fruits he will gather in a future life. Giving is thus an essential duty of the head of the house, but he interprets it in different terms from ours. A sort of moral code, written in Tamil, the *Tirukkural*, expounds the duty of giving in these words: 'That you are asked for alms is painful until you see the smiling face of the satisfied beggar' (i.xxiii. 222). One could take it for a general statement not unlike what could be heard in a Western country. But this maxim is sandwiched between two others which run as follows: 'Even if one is solemnly assured that it leads direct to heaven, a gift received is bad; and even if the existence of heaven is denied, to give is good'; and: 'For the ascetic true will-power resides in over-coming the sufferings of hunger. For the head of a house to allay the hunger of the holy ascetic by giving him food is the highest act of virtue and nothing can compare with it.' Which might be insufficiently compelling if the following maxim did not elaborate: 'To allay the hunger of the holy ascetic who has renounced everything is the exact equivalent of putting one's own fortune in a safe place.' The *sadhu*

is the only person who can take a gift without being degraded by it, because his very presence is a blessing, and a gift to a *sadhu* is the only form of meritorious almsgiving. In this idea of an exchange of services one recognizes a very archaic conception of social relations; giving is, as it were, a luxury, a sign of the wealth which permits of liberality. A 'good' Hindu beggar, for that matter, is perfectly well aware of the fact and, not wishinq to be in your debt or humiliated when he accepts alms, showers blessings on you. Further, you must never refuse him money harshly but, on the contrary, apologise for giving nothing, under penalty of being cursed.

So, though the impulse of the heart is generally lacking, the result is much the same. This conception of giving is so deeply ingrained that I once heard a Brahman, to whom the Christian idea of the creation of the world was being described as a gift from God, exclaim: 'Come, come! God can't make a gift; it would mean He expected something in return.' But, when all is said and done, in this conception there is something that guarantees normal social exchanges: the whole caste system is conceived as one vast exchange, and the diversity of the marriage laws has the sole aim of preserving families intact, at any rate economically; the woman who gives a daughter must receive one for her son. This is the whole significance of inter-marriages between cousins – with the daughter of the maternal uncle or sometimes of the paternal aunt – a custom still very much in force today in the South; or again, of the hypergamous marriages of the North, where a wife for the son is sought in the immediately lower caste in exchange for which the daughter is married into the caste immediately above. By the same token, you could say, if I receive a wage I have to give work in exchange, and if I work for nothing, I am assured of a position superior to those for whom I have done the favour.

Possibly at the back of one's mind there is also the idea that a people so religious as the Indians are unable to submit themselves to purely economic imperatives, to think in economic terms. Actually I know of no people more adept at mixing the sacred and the profane, perhaps precisely because the whole of Indian culture is based on their indivisibility. The predominance of religion has never prevented the Hindu, within the framework of his caste, from thinking in a very profane manner, whether as artisan or tradesman. One also tends to forget, or does not know, that Indian society too, despite its well-established hierarchy, has experience of what might be called social demands, which the ruler tried to satisfy when they came from the trading or artisan castes, representing the wealth of the country. To take one case, Vijayanagar's empire in the 15th century offers many examples of precisely this kind, strongly reminiscent of the emancipation of some Western European bourgeoisies in the Middle Ages.

To the sceptics who consider the Indian incapable of adapting himself to modern conditions of work because for centuries past he has used the same tools without improvements, one can reply quite definitely: to some extent it was the Muslim invasions which, in many instances, put a stop to the development of ancient techniques; certainly this applies to architecture and sculpture, which were never renewed by the Hindus except in the southern areas which had escaped destruction, as the ruins of Vijayanagar, the great temple and palace of Madura, bear witness. In the 18th century, Indian textiles were in great demand, not only in Africa and in other parts of Asia, but very soon in Europe too. At that time India was in hardly any respect behind Europe. And this was the more to its credit, considering the troubled life, and one of appalling insecurity, that its various masters forced it to lead. Silks, cottons, and the famous muslins were very properly admired.

And, above all, why is one so sure that improvement of technique is always possible and desirable? There are economists who hold, for example, that the wooden swing-plough, the only working implement which the Indian peasant has ever known, is the most suited to the soil, at least in the vast areas where the arable top-soil is rather shallow and where scraping the underlying rock with a metal ploughshare would destroy the earth's fertility. And who knows what the Indian peasant could have done had he not, like the towns and the fortresses, been at the mercy of warriors and of extreme poverty over long ages? Generally speaking, and ever since the possibility existed, he has always been prohibited, to all intents and purposes, from buying new seed, or manure, not to speak of better implements; his land was too poor, or too restricted in area, or too saddled with debts. There was a time, under the

'The famous muslin

Mughals, when fifty per cent of the crops went to the emperor.

And yet, in Kerala, well known for its rich soil, but where the density of population is so great that there is a continuous emigration, I have seen peasants cultivating a lateritic hillside, which nobody could have wanted: they were growing cassava, their staple crop, the yield being a fifth of that from the fertile soil of East Kerala, at the foot of the Ghats. They were also planting trees. Their industry and ingenuity were only equalled, however, by their poverty; they did not even eat every day.

Sometimes one will see slopes with furrows cut from top to bottom, which encourages erosion during the monsoon. This argues an ignorance that could very certainly be remedied. Representatives in India of European chemical fertilizer manufacturers are well aware of this, for they go about teaching the peasants how to improve the produce of their fields and make them cultivate new crops, and in every village they come across people who want to know more, generally amongst those with a bit more land. In any case, it should not be forgotten that in a tropical country there are certain limits, both as regards methods and yields, which cannot be exceeded.

As for industrialization, everyone knows why it was not undertaken earlier. But is it known, for example, that a few years ago a group of Indian textile workers went to France to work side by side with French workers? The comparison tended to be to the Indian workers' advantage. There is no question that when it comes to manual dexterity they are second to none.

. . . And real ones

My purpose was to prove that the Indians are capable of adapting themselves to the new conditions of life to which they are subjected, even though these are very different from anything they have known before and even though they belong to those Oriental peoples whom some are so ready to consign to perpetual poverty and the most complete social immutability. But, you may say, why go to so much trouble to prove that it *should* go well, when in fact it leaves so much to be desired? All right: the people are capable of adapting themselves, but everything tends to slow up progress and make it painful. Yes, I have to acknowledge that here our concealed racialists seem to be getting the best of it; like all Eastern countries, India is a prey to disorganization, to appalling inefficiency and to riotous corruption. Engineers returning from America or Europe, where they were in many cases brilliant as students, are no sooner home than they sink back into the rut; they become specialists in minimum output again. Office workers beat all records for indolence, and when you visit a government department you are almost unable to believe your eyes if you find anyone at work. It should be added that a clerk's job in one of these offices is the most sought after: it means a small wage, but security and practically no work. In 1956, after the yearly examinations had been held, the employment exchanges complained that they had only 200 or 300 places to offer 10,000 candidates, all of whom, on leaving secondary schools, and even universities, wanted to be clerks. There were not enough shorthand typists to go round, even fewer stenotypists, accountants, and so on, but none of these youngsters seeking employment could be bothered to specialize.

At a lower level, you find the same problem and the same trouble; servants and workers dream of becoming 'peons', something rather like our messengers in government departments. India already employs a tremendous number of these. They are paid very little and do practically nothing, but probably for those who hanker for this type of job it is their only means of avoiding manual labour, which is traditionally looked down upon. It is not only that the thing you work with may be unclean; what you do may also be degrading, for example, to stoop to the ground. The European agricultural experts to whom I referred have one infallible way of arousing the peasants' lively interest, namely, by setting to work, turning up the soil and putting in plants. For a *sahib* to stoop to the ground like that must mean a very important or highly lucrative return.

The inefficiency with which things are done is quite unbelievable: omissions, mistakes, files lost and never found again are the commonest occurrences. I have had to wait a whole hour at a post office counter where the clerk was absent and no one, not even his chief, knew where he was.

Daily Rice

I had to leave before he reappeared. Not that this is the prerogative of office workers alone: the craftsmen are nothing about 'good workmanship', and everyone in India knows that if you want a decent pair of shoes you had better go to a Chinese shoemaker. The factory-produced goods are generally of poor quality; and why not say so since the papers are full of these facts?

Recently there was talk again of trade with the United States: India would export handwoven textiles, but there would be a special quality inspection before despatch. One Indian firm producing sewing-machines has opened up a vast market in the Far East. Because its markets are assured, it lowers – whether passively or actively – the quality of its products. Does anyone eat unadulterated butter? Does

anyone get medicaments exactly according to the prescription? People express surprise when a supposedly potent pill has no effect; on analysis such a harmless concoction is revealed that nobody could have expected anything of it. A man dies suddenly after having taken the stipulated dose of a certain remedy; it turns out to have been two hundred times stronger than it should have been. Which explains why all Westerners living in India, and a large number of Indians as well, are obsessed by imported products, which are expensive but dependable. The balance of trade suffers in consequence, so the government imposes restrictions and promises to keep an eye on the quality of Indian products. But how can this be done effectively when the whole administration especially the police, can be bought? There

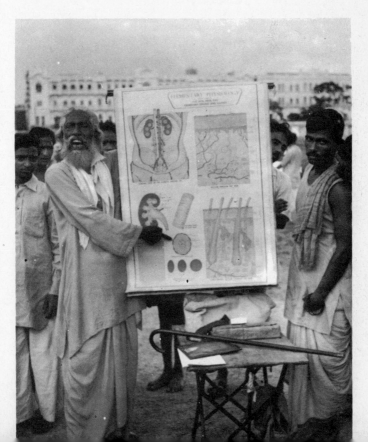

is a sort of link between apathy and corruption; they are like two facets of the same evil which must live or die together.

I am not sure that I know the full extent of this corruption. I am always discovering new spheres where it works its havoc, even though as a European I am relatively immune to it. It is no secret, and from time to time the newspapers themselves come out and denounce it. Periodically, and in particular near election times, the Congress declares war on this public evil. I shall cite only a few examples, too well known to be challenged, and I shall not select them from the political sphere, which might make some Western voters laugh. In a country where underemployment is chronic, there is naturally a black market in jobs; people know that such and such a position costs 300 rupees, another 500, and so on, and no one feels the smallest surprise. It is far more surprising that there are still applicants to appear before the appointment boards of this bank or that government department in the hope of obtaining a vacant position. Generally the candidate has been selected before the board meets, and is not always to be found amongst the applicants. The most serious aspect of this practice is obviously that the question of ability does not enter into the matter, and thus the present evil is perpetuated. But what about the hospital where you cannot receive treatment without first distributing rupees to everybody from the head doctor to the hall porter? It would be nice to think that this is an exceptional case.

The Indians do not deny the evil; nor do they acquiesce in it, for too often they are its victims. The victory of the Communists in Kerala in 1957 is only one, but the most important, witness to the fact: Communists and non-Communists, with the exception of the Catholics, voted as one man against the Congress which had allowed corruption to flourish and had widely profited by it; they voted for the only party which seemed determined to wage war to the bitter end against corruption, wherever it lurked. I happened to be in Trivandrum, the capital of Kerala, just when the results of the 1957 elections were coming in day by day from the rural constituencies. I met a good many devont Hindus there, religious men and loyal followers of this *guru* or that *asram*, whose liberal opinions and ascetic tastes hardly predisposed them to social protest. Nevertheless they had all voted Communist and looked to their elected members to cleanse the air.

Yet whenever I ask who or what is responsible for this state of affairs, the Indians reply in chorus and without a moment's hesitation: the British. For a long time I thought that the British were a slightly too convenient scapegoat and that they were rather too hastily blamed for everything wrong with India since its independence. I was the more confirmed in my scepticism by the fact that corruption in all its forms was already flourishing at the time of the Mughals; and how could it have been otherwise when the rulers of the day set the example themselves, buying their enemies' retainers in order to triumph more surely over them? The law as administered in the provinces was as venal as it was accommodating, so much so that in one district in the North the saying ran: 'When the Kazi's mistress dies, everyone goes to her funeral; when the Kazi himself dies, nobody bothers.' So, I said to myself, how can the British be responsible, they who set up a more honest administration than many another? And yet the charge is not so far off the truth; the British together with the Mughals are in large part responsible for the present corruption, as also, if it comes to that, for the disorganization and inefficiency. When, for centuries, public welfare has been identified with the will and pleasure of a foreign ruler, it is difficult to see how a sturdy civic spirit could have been developed.

To which must be added the enormous disparity of salaries, originally introduced by the Mughals and perpetuated by the British, and no doubt by all colonizers; the situation in India today which I am trying to describe is very much like that in many other countries recently liberated from the colonial yoke. Under the Mughal emperor there were a great many officials who received the equivalent of 30,000 to 40,000 rupees a month, while the highest paid artisan earned less than a rupee a day. The British reduced the discrepancies quite considerably but there was still an unbridgeable gap between the 2,000 rupees of the most lowly British official and his servant's 30 or 40 rupees. And the office-worker of today is on a par with the servant and the artisan. He belongs to one of the worst-paid categories in Indian society, even if the rate is relatively variable. His money-troubles are ceaseless; he tries to dress better than the office-boy and also he has children whom

he would like to send to school and even to college, though he has not the means to do so. Where in the world would you not find, in such circumstances, a measure of slovenliness and corruption?

But I believe that in this case the evil has even deeper roots. Officialdom and the whole structure of a modern society are still very new to the Indian. They do not fit into the traditional framework of a caste society, which lays down what he must and what he must not do and provides him with a complete ethico-religious code to guide him. Money is not in that situation the most essential thing, nor even the most precious. But, transposed into a money economy, the Indian is more liable than anyone else, perhaps, to lose his head. He is very easily intoxicated by this new source of social prestige and material comfort. He envies his superior who treats him harshly. Let me say again, the caste system does not encourage purely human impulses, either of sympathy or even of pity; the tendency when faced by someone even poorer than oneself is to take the utmost advantage of it. That is, in fact, what the usurer in traditional Indian society did. I realizes the gravity of what I am saying and I am weighing my words carefully. I know, having lived, and still living, in this country which I am trying to describe, how Western countries appear in the eyes of other nations and how severely we are judged. Nevertheless it must be said that in our countries there is at least a quality of humanity in our personal and working relations which is too often lacking here.

I say this without overlooking the very noble exceptions to be met in India, who would furnish proof, if we had need of it, of the universality of human nature and of the fact that good and evil look alike everywhere. But we are more the products of civilization than of nature. In an environment where hard-heartedness and oppression of the weak are not frowned upon by public opinion, it is inevitable that there should be an almost wholesale drive for money and position, the sources of prestige. The hierarchy of caste was as much a form of protection as a system of discrimination. In the setting of modern life and a money economy, the weak are more vulnerable than ever. But India is still at the stage of feeling intoxicated by having free play, which is natural enough. In fact, it is those who, having come from low castes, from habitually downtrodden social strata, have now acceded to a little power, however pitiful, who show themselves most ruthless and greedy. Growing pains, the discovery of freedom both for good and for evil – all this disequilibrium will be righted with the years. The new conditions of urban life, in particular, create an atmosphere in which people are not able to recognize others as their fellow-men, in which new values have to come into being and gradually replace the old.

At the present time there is a tide of sincerity and honesty running, owing to the new fiscal policy introduced by the government to finance the Second Five Year Plan. It has aroused high feeling, as much in the ranks of the privileged, threatened by a new tax on wealth, as amongst the people, already suffering from the beginnings of inflation; new indirect taxes and the lowering of the minimum taxable income weigh heavily on millions of small wage-earners in India. Naturally, Parliament reflects the impact of these measures and there is a crossfire of criticism and counter-criticism, of proposals and counter-proposals. But out of this welter of opinions, there are two points on which all parties are unanimous, Congress included. First and foremost, on the outrageous extravagance of certain leading figures and the prestige-spending which they seem to think necessary. The leader of the P.S.P. (Praja Socialist Party) related in great detail at a session of the Lower House the luxurious reception he had been given by one of the State Governors. A Communist Member referred to the Governor of Punjab's palace, being built at a cost of 4 million rupees while the Untouchables have not so much as a roof over their heads. The fact is that the Indians, and not only their leaders, have a tendency, like many southern peoples, to believe that their authority will go unrecognized if they do not enhance their prestige by conspicuous waste. Can this be a hangover of potlatch? So now it is proposed to axe this luxury spending, to reduce the salaries of higher officials and ministers receiving over 2,000 rupees a month (a worker, that is to say – as we shall see – a rather privileged person, earns between 80 and 100 rupees, which should be compared with the difference between similar categories in our countries); they are to issue slightly fewer invitations to foreigners and send slightly fewer Indian delegations abroad. The second point on which there is unanimity is even more interesting: the cost of projects included in the

Plan is far too high and constantly mounting: 'No one denies that there is corruption and inefficiency in their execution,' said someone in the Lower House, and he calculated that there could be a saving of 10 per cent on the estimated expense. Shortly after this the lack of coordination between the various aspects of the Plan was also brought to light. It was found that the energy generated by the newly constructed dams was not being fully used.

One might take this as a plain case of 'washing dirty linen.' Myself, I do not think so. India, after all, wanted a democratic regime and has not the means of exercising long-term restraints, of increasing austerity for the people, once opinion is thus well informed. It would be very surprising if amongst the members of Parliament who thus indulged in an examination of their consciences (on behalf of the government) there were not some who had taken bribes, not some who had pocketed a little something from public funds, particularly amongst the representatives of the party in power. Here, too, it is neither more nor less than their own future that is at stake. The corruption of the Congress Party is well known and cannot last forever. It seems therefore that for the time being they are in the trough of the wave. As in all nationalist parties throughout the world, the achievement of independence is bound to go to the heads of quite a few. And at least in India that party has not vested itself with the means of perpetuating itself in power.

What, then, was the upshot of that memorable session of home truths? Day by day the papers reported that the Ministers of this or that State had asked for a reduction of salary, and that some other official had relinquished his salary (which does not suggest, of course, that he and his entire family intended to starve to death, but, on the contrary, that he had other and possibly more handsome means of subsistence than his salary. The atmosphere proved so stimulating to splendid gestures and so contagious that Le Corbusier was the first in Punjab – where he was building the new capitol – to demand reduction of fees. And all this

Daily Rice

in order to effect economies which would help to finance the Plan. One may have doubts as to the efficacy of the movement, which is of more or less the same character as the agrarian reforms proposed by Vinoba Bhave. Will it suffice, not only to raise the funds required, but to stem corruption and the diversion of public money? There is, however, no doubt that public opinion has reacted favourably – and awaits results.

But the moral transformation can only, alas, be very slow. So long as poverty allows consciences to be bought for a few rupees, there is little chance of a radical change in the situation. Will the country have the patience to wait for tangible results? That is the whole question. And will India succeed in overcoming the appalling scourges which afflict it – under-employment, the deficiency and irregularity of agricultural produce, famines and epidemics – while pur-

Worker in the Kolar Goldmines

The Bhakra-Nangal Dam

suing the policy it has mapped out for itself? How far has it gone? How far, confronted by so many obstacles, will the Plans take it?

There is a positive side to the picture: over many decades of working-class struggle in our countries in the West, the proletariat has come to be identified with the factory worker. No doubt, if one sticks to a Marxist definition of the term, the industrial worker in India is a proletarian too, but compared with so many of his compatriots in the countryside, or those employed as servants and petty clerks, he is positively the 'new rich.' His 80 to 100 rupees a month ensure that he gets enough to eat. He benefits by the Union or State social legislation which in itself accords him a privileged position: statutory working hours, a minimum

wage, welfare centres, and annual holidays on the basis of one day for every twenty working days in addition to Sundays. In some large factories in the North a pension scheme has been introduced which prevents the super-annuated worker from being wholly dependent upon his family. I know full well that I have always visited factories in the company of managers and that they could have been pulling the wool over my eyes (but not to any great extent; The colour of my skin was enough to inspire them with confidence: I could not help being on their side, of course); and I do not deny that there are many factories well away from the main industrial centres which do not carry out the regulations and cannot be forced to do so by a trade union owing to the surplus manpower. Nor is there any reason to conceal that my blood ran cold when one of these big factory bosses, referring to the union associated with Congress (for all the large unions are officially attached to one or more of the political parties), said: 'Oh, yes, it's on our side (the employers). It shows a lot of understanding and you can always make it listen to reason.' All the conditions are there for a working-class struggle to develop in the years to come. Nevertheless, I cannot forget those decently dressed workers pouring out of the factory gates, who made me sigh with relief after coming from the villages with their half-starved inhabitants. In the factories where I have been the tempo of work does not give the impression of hell let loose which I had, for instance, a few years ago in a Czech factory. The men do not seem to be killing themselves with work and it is a fair bet that they find conditions more humane than in their village communities. They would certainly think so if they had all come from the most miserable sections of the rural population, which is not the case.

But the life of the urban worker is by no means a bed of roses. His trade union may be strong, as those controlled by the Communists and Socialists are, but it has not yet managed to find him a decent dwelling. There are some successful schemes, such as that of the Tata plant at Jamshedpur, where the worker is given accommodation at the same time as a job, and a few other exceptional cases, advertised by the Indians *urbi et orbi*. But as a whole it is a system of shanty towns that prevails. The horror of these rows or huddles of rusty sheet-metal shacks is difficult to express, but anyone who knows almost any part of Africa will hardly require a description. They are not much more hideous in India, but their total discomfort is aggravated by the yearly monsoon; the rainy season witnesses the death of old people and young children, the spread of disease and the exacerbation of misery; at those times the inhabitants live with their feet in water and have difficulty in keeping their clothes dry. So far the influx of new workers has only succeeded in multiplying these landscapes of desolation surrounding the industrial centres, and nothing, or next to nothing, has been done to house the thousands of uprooted people. The working-class population is, indeed, relatively so small that the authorities' failure should not cause too much astonishment; class-consciousness has barely emerged and the trade unions are only just beginning to make their voice heard. Added to which the government, bent on encouraging investment, is unable to exercise pressure on the capitalists in this matter as in many others.

But it is in the countryside that you can see India striving towards a better life. The pace of industrialization is not such that it will very rapidly depopulate the villages for the benefit of the towns. There is not much that can be said about the land reform, which, like everything else, is to be carried out under the banner of freedom. The various States have reached different stages of it, but nowhere is the reform complete, not even where the big landowners have been dispossessed. Kerala's attempt to go further – immediately opposed by the Union Government – is the clearest sign that nothing very far-reaching can be expected in this field; here it was a question of nationalizing foreign-owned tea plantations, as a first step no doubt. It seems that any move of this kind was contrary to the spirit of the Indian Constitution.

On the other hand, the Government had thought of including in the Second Five Year Plan Vinoba Bhave's campaign, a fairly cheap counter with which it could have paid tribute to the memory of Gandhi, whose name Bhave invokes. Certainly India is the only country where any such scheme could have seen the light of day; the idea is to ask those who own land to give it, of their own free will, to those who have none. But at the same time we should beware of thinking that India is the country where such ideas succeed. The goals set by Bhave have never been reached; so far from it that the sponsors have given up presenting figures, and confine themselves to describing the enthusiasm of the masses. Some people complain that the land thus acquired is of poor quality and that the big land-owners generously give what is of no use to them. And how else could it be? In any case, the disciple's moves are very far from rousing the whole people in the way that the Master's slightest gesture did. Is it a lack of breadth in the Mahratta apostle? Is it the apathy of the masses, who have fallen back again into their age-old misery after the vague hopes aroused by the Mahatma? Or is it perhaps that they understand clearly enough that the redistribution of land is no solution when that land has to feed 30 million useless people? Shortly after the accession of the Communists in Kerala, Bhave turned up with his followers and predicted, in the presence of the officials who had come to welcome him, that he would bring about the land reform of the country more quickly than the Government. There are no signs that his predictions are about to be fulfilled; but what is evident is that, paradoxically, he is meeting with exactly the same obstacles as an authoritarian regime would encounter in trying to introduce co-operative farming; the Indian peasant is not ready for this form of working the land. The government of Kerala, until its removal on July 31st, 1959, was distributing small parcels of the land which it had at its disposal to the most needy and was meeting with far greater enthusiasm, as well as better yields.

But the real spirit of Gandhi – which I should prefer to call the real Indian genius – is to be found elsewhere. Why do it the disservice of identifying it with methods whose utupian and ineffectual character has already been proved? No. Let us rather look for it in what is being done in the villages, where thousands of anonymous workers are striving to educate an ignorant population on the spot. The government has few illusions about the rate at which economic conditions will improve, so it encourages those who, making the best of a bad job, try to turn the present state of things to good account and to help others to do likewise. Amongst these anonymous and dedicated people some explicitly associate themselves with the Mahatma, such as the 'Sarvo-daya workers' (those who work to elevate everyone). Truth compels me to admit that at the present time these are the least effective; but others are completely independent of Gandhi, thus proving that what is best in his methods is primarily and in essence Indian. What Gandhi did was to systematize and render effective attitudes of mind latent in the best of his countrymen; his originality resided in the courage with which he applied his ideas – which were pretty vague, when all is said and done – down to the last detail of the daily necessities of life.

There are people who build and maintain roads and bridges and public buildings with which they try to endow the villages at small cost; and, above all, there are those who, living entirely with the peasants, patiently seek to educate the children, teach the women how to sew and knit and, more particularly, to mend. Everything has still to be learnt, from a few rules of hygiene to the alphabet. Perhaps my European standards of comfort have made me naive, but I marvelled at the ingenuity displayed, not only to arouse the interest of the people – which is often the hardest part of the job – but to make something out of nothing. The means are so slender, the results often amazing. Match factories are built to provide employment for the women, men are taught to use the weaving loom, the handloom which may give back to Indian textiles their international reputation. But here again the use of the spinning-wheel and loom is not bound up with the ideology of ging back to the handicraft stage of development; the cottage industries are part of the solution to the problems of transition; partial solutions, unfortunately, to the problem of unemployment and under-employment, until industry is sufficiently developed. Their contribution is not to be sneezed at. Rural life is so simple and so cheap that a few extra rupees a month are enough to alleviate distress, if not poverty.

The poetry and the great beauty of that simplicity is beyond my powers of description. The weavers at work under the coconut palms or banyan trees stretch their brightly coloured threads for the woof of the *dhotis* and *saris* they are going to weave; with deft and lively movements they mix and separate the variegated colours on which flecks of sunlight play. A woman washes herself, without soap, squatting by a pitcher of warm water, she rubs her skin and her sari at the same time, not forgetting her hair, which she sprinkles plentifully from a cup *(lota)* filled at the pitcher; she combs her hair unhurriedly with her fingers, and the result is unexpectedly pleasing. The whole

Daily Rice

performance takes the best part of an hour. While this is going on, the potters are at their wheels, the housewives are wielding their brushwood brooms all round the coconut matting or bamboo huts. People seated ·on the ground eat with their fingers from a piece of banana leaf or a copper vessel; a change of clothes – when there is one – is hung on a line stretched across the interior of the hut. Everyone drinks from the single copper mug, without letting his lips touch it. In the summer people sleep in the open, on the ground, lying on very comfortable rope beds, which cost 4 rupees – about 6/— or 11 cents – so that this in itself is something of a luxury. Children appear from everywhere,

completely naked in the South as a rule and in the North wearing trousers and flowing shirts of the most varied styles. When they have enough to eat they are generally lovely; their eyes and smiles enchant you at first sight.

As soon as a village has taken up one or more handicrafts in this way and no longer depends wholly on the land – unless, in exceptional cases, there happens to be enough of it – it is practically saved and everything breathes a kind of carefreeness, outside time, outside history. Outside history, yes, indeed! Once, in the course of a conversation with a Nayyar who owned rice-fields and coconut palms – a mark of affluence – I was well able to observe that his knowledge of events was a trifle out of date. He knew that Nehru was something at the peak of the government pyramid, which not everyone knows. He had once, under the British·occupation, gone with some other workers to help in the building of the strategic road from India to Burma. His knowledge of the rest of the world dated from that time; in 1951 he thought Roosevelt was still alive and of course he had not heard any talk about a third world war. I do not know what independence meant to him, but it is certain that it could not have represented more than a minimal change in his life and his outlook.

But how many people are there still without any means of support? You could count them by the number of children with swollen bellies due to malnutrition; by those rachitic and silent children who, when they were at their mothers' breasts, were beautiful babies; by those gaunt old men who gaze at you, shivering despite the heat; by those idlers sitting under a tree, chewing betel-nut, who seem to have been waiting for you since the beginning of time. These are the common sights of the Indian countryside and all the devoted efforts in the world will not suffice to find them new means of subsistence.

Naturally, at the village level you find the chronic disease of the towns again: inefficiency coupled with corruption. Where unemployment is rife, any job is a good job. The great majority of those who work for the revival of the villages gladly accept the wage – small but not negligible – since it is this or nothing; they are equally ready to handle the public funds entrusted to them for distribution expenses, and one can guess the result. Even those who are called 'social workers' generally have no special aptitude for tracking down leprosy-sufferers and other duties of the sort. I have heard more than one Hindu deplore the fact that his religion had not set up charitable institutions similar to those in Europe, religious organizations dedicated to the care of the sick and social outcasts of every kind. The Ramakrishna Mission, which within Hinduism comes nearest to gratifying this wish, does not deny that in fact it owes the origins of its social work to Christian influences.

But, even supposing that everything were for the best, the devotion and integrity of all concerned would not be enough to create work for the legions of the unemployed of today and those who, each year, will join them as the population increases. The fact is that the Five Year Plans, in their present form, are powerless to absorb this manpower. The liberal policy, the almost complete absence of pressure on capital, combined with the reluctance of foreign capital (a further result of India's ambiguous policy), mean that industrialization will be very sow. Indian economists are agreed that it will be very difficult to prevent unemployment from growing; the Plans to come will only just succeed in providing an additional 1,800,000 new jobs, an increase which corresponds with the increase of population. The text of the present Plan makes this clear. And even the carrying out of the Plans depends on the assumption that the difficulties of financing them will not produce inflation. Yet inflation is already making itself felt, with its train of wage demands and the fresh rise in prices resulting from them. Some favour the government's taking over the trade in essential foodstuffs; but any such measure would be contrary to official liberalism and would not prevent a rise in the price of cement, steel and other raw materials needed for equipping the country.

It is the admittedly limited scope of the Plan's objectives – still considered too bold by some financial experts – which has caused the Government to branch out in a new field. Fortunately for it, China has recently started a vigorous campaign for birth control, which has effectively silenced the Left opposition. The time is past when such barbarous ideas as sterilization were looked upon as bourgeois ideology. A great Communist country has admitted that, at any rate for the time being, it cannot possibly cope with the increase of its population. The Indian Government wavered for a long time. Birth-control propaganda was already in full

swing in the country while it was refused official sanction.
But now the second Plan includes the setting up of 'family-
planning clinics' almost everywhere; the instruction of women
on this matter is part of the village 'basic education'. While
they are being taught to sew, it is put to them that they
already have more than enough children, that they should
be operated on to prevent a further increase in the family.
I recently had the privilege of being introduced to an Indian

woman justly famed for having prevented the birth of 15,000 children. (The presumption of statistics!) I must, however, in all truth add that the new policy of birth control has little effect except on couples, mostly town dwellers, who could in fact afford to bring up large families. What is more, in a country where women, by their own wish, exercise less initiative than they do in our countries, you can hear this sort of thing said, as I did one day: 'I've two children as it is, that's quite enough; so I've had my wife operated on.' Amongst the emancipated section of the population this seems the last word in Civilization. But amongst the villagers, the reply elicited by the instructors is invariably: 'If we have more children, God will look after them.' There have already been terrible scenes over operations done without the women's knowledge by doctors who systematically sterilized them after a certain number of parturitions. Indian democracy, paradoxically enough, does not interpret freedom on this point in the same terms as we do. I was told about a village where thirty men were sterilized in one go, representing the entire male population above a given age. But, despite happenings of this kind, I believe that the mystique of sterility will penetrate popular consciousness even more slowly than the letters of the alphabet.

Future

So it is not a glowing situation, far from it. For a long time to come there will be talk in India of famine, of monsoons which fail to come or come too early, bringing catastrophe, if only locally, in their wake. I have tried to make allowances for the actual economic policy by showing its inherent limitations. But would a more authoritarian, a more totalitarian policy — bringing other evils in its train — resolve the problems of the day any better? Or more quickly? It has been a dogma of the extreme Left that, the means of subsistence being susceptible of indefinite increase and the whole matter being one of political organization, there is no such thing as an overpopulated country, no such thing as a country that cannot feed its population. This is apparently no longer the case in China. And in India? In absolute figures you cannot even say that it is overpopulated, the average density of population being in the region of 287 per square mile. (In the United Kingdom it is 770 and in the United States 51). Why then is it so poverty-stricken? Why can one not foresee the day when it will no longer be so? All these questions torment you, because your mind refuses to find the answer. The solution is perhaps not solely political, or at least does not perhaps arise purely from India's internal policy. Since it has begun to be said that tropical areas are at a disadvantage compared to others, and more particularly that agricultural production cannot be indefinitely increased, the Indian Government has taken up the rumour and used it as an excuse. The last Census Report noted that Indian agriculture cannot and never will suffice to feed the sub-continent. It could be argued that this takes too little account of the wealth of the soil and the subsoil in minerals of all sorts, of which thorium and uranium, sources of almost unlimited energy, are still unworked and will remain so for a long time to come.

It is not for me to settle the question. The fact is that Indian policy favours the slow and relatively broad way of economic freedom rather than the steep path of compulsion. But it is also true that the nation is gradually being won over by official slogans. Nehru's international standing, his role at Bandung, and the support he gives to the young Afro-Asian nationalist movements, have earned him, in this field, the blind allegiance of the entire people, not least that of the Communists. But the people's confidence goes perhaps deeper still: round about 1950 I should have been quite ready to compare the power of Congress to that of the Kuomintang and Nehru to Chiang Kai-Shek. The Communists were making enormous progress on the Malabar Coast in the South; they had taken power in a small corner of the prevent State of Andhra and were running it in their own way. Although Communist Kerala was suffered to exist only between April 1957 and July 1959, it could not have been regarded as a second Yenan. The huge State of Madras adjoining it elected only 5 Communist members to the State Assembly and there is little likelihood that the example of the neighbouring State will prove infectious in the short run, particularly if Indian Communism wants to go on gaining ground by parliamentary means; and it is difficult to see what else it can do at the present time. In any case, it is possible for anyone to believe that the Communist danger was responsible for Nehru's socialist leap in recent years; and the electoral setback for the Congress Party in Kerala, Maharashtra, and Orissa was no doubt owing to the reformation which was going on at the time inside the Party in power in Delhi.

But while the Communists, in village and factory, are only out to stir up revolt and demands, the authorities, despite inefficiency and corruption, are making an effort to get something done. Everybody has the feeling that things are on the move, even though they are moving slowly. People are waiting; they are prepared to go on trusting the regime and the Congress Party for a while. Let us try to summon up again, if we still can, our fervour of 1944–45. Something of this sort prevails amongst the articulate minority of the Indian population: for the first time in living memory what is going on in this country is not being done for the benefit of a foreign nation; the young people being trained in the universities will serve an Indian administration; the dams and bridges being built will give the country the modern equipment which will enable it to bear comparison with technically advanced nations.

I disappointed many fellow travellers whom I met in the train by telling them that I had been to Banaras (Benares) but had not visited the Damodar Valley Project, that I had admired the Vijayanagar ruins but had not deigned to cover the few extra kilometres to see the Tungabadra dam. The Indian looks at a dam in construction and the complicated machinery in a factory with a child's wonderment. But make no mistake; his delight is less that of a primitive man than that of someone who has too long been deprived of these things, as of a forbidden toy. He learns very quickly to harness them for his own purposes, to understand a useful piece of machinery and reject a useless one, such as the cranes in the port of Bombay, which would have taken work from the dockers. The men in power, who have brought about so many changes in the country, are venerated for it. Gratitude pours out to them, without having been openly solicited.

The fact is that there is no All-Indian Party which would be ready to take over power. In places where the Congress Party lost the last elections – apart from Kerala – it was coalitions of Parties or the local State Parties which got in: a coalition in favour of the separation of Maharashtra

and Gujarat in the present State of Bombay; Dravida Kazhagam, or the Dravidian Party of Madras State, in favour of the secession of the South of India. In Orissa, where Congress only just got in, and not without some manoeuvring, its main opponent was a Right Wing local Party. None of these parties put forward a positive programme of government. Can the Congress Party really be considered in danger from these almost non-political groupings?

And why criticize the slowness of development in India? Or, more precisely, why hold it against the Congress government? It is not at all certain that the mass of the Indian people think in these terms. The upheavals they have experienced are possibly as much as they can stand at a time, and the present slow measure may well be precisely the tempo that suits them. The wisdom of the people may reside in wanting to go forward at their own pace, gently and with the minimum turmoil. I advance this view with due cautiousness, but I know I shall draw fire. What do you mean? People who are dying of hunger are in no hurry to eat their fill? Yes, of course, if that were the only thing, but more plentiful food would also entail wholesale changes in a way of life. The chronic drought, the roofs which let in rain set up their own routines from which it is not easy to tear oneself. The transformation can only take place slowly, down below as up above.

And I come back to an idea I cherish: this leisurely pace, which would be intolerable to our made-in-Europe or made-in-America susceptibilities, is probably necessary if India is to remain India, or even simply a humane country, and not just become a poor imitation of a Western country; so many time-honoured institutions would have to give way that a profound disequilibrium could well result. You do not put new wine in old bottles; a new mentality must be allowed to germinate slowly in contact with new realities, a new ethical structure which will order the Hindu's new universe. What will that structure be?

Shanti

'WHAT IS YOUR RELIGION?' That is the second question I am generally asked on a train, the first being 'Where do you come from?' I don't think I have been quite fair up to now about the Hindu attitude, which is so religious, so convinced that one must have a religion. It would not matter in the least if I replied, 'I am a Muslim,' or 'I worship the sun,' so long as I do not say, 'I have no religion,' or 'I do not believe in God.' These latter answers are beyond comprehension and arouse nothing but faintly disdainful surprise. Nowadays, in the destructive atmosphere of the cities, one does begin to meet people apparently without any beliefs; they are for the most part not very successful people and they are the exception. The Hindu, however detached from his caste, from caste practices and beliefs, however much a stranger to the temples, will go on calling himself a Hindu and talking of God, with a capital letter, in every sentence. The emotions of people who are utterly without scruple in their working life are very quickly touched if you draw them on to walk about religion. Hinduism, as we have already conjectured, is not quite the same thing as caste, that social system which, as we have seen, is destined to wither away gradually.

We are faced with a total paradox, I am almost tempted to say a total contradiction; if I have not referred to the other facet of Hinduism until now, it is because it seemed to me impossible not to see a profound gulf between the religion of caste and the pursuit of salvation as India has conceived it over thousands of years. No doubt this parting of the ways is owing to the diversity of historical currents which have merged into modern Hinduism. Perhaps there was a Vedic religion, in love with life and earthly goods, on to which the Upanishad revolution, roughly contemporary with Buddhism, was grafted; a revolution which joined on to something else and did not destroy it. I am conscious of the incongruity, but how else to describe Hindu and thereby Indian reality? The Upanishads, the series of sacred books spanning a period of over ten centuries which traversed the beginning of the Christian era, do not by any means form a homogeneous whole. But they reach modern consciousness mainly through the interpretation of their essentials by the philosopher Sankara in the 9th century: the whole universe is the sum of phenomena which have no reality of their own; it is illusion, and that term is to be understood in its fullest sense; the *maya* of the god Indra is the magic power by which he causes unreal things to appear in order to deceive his enemies; it is, quite precisely, his power as an illusionist. For Sankara *maya* is the projection of manifold and various phenomena against the background of a perfect Absolute. There is something akin to original sin which, from birth onwards, makes us unaware of the unity of all things and of the ultimate reality in which all differences are dissolved; the will to be saved thus coincides with the effort to attain to knowledge of this reality – *Sat,* Being.

We are thus dealing with an outlook on the world which, on the one hand, accepts an infinity of rebirths through castes and centuries, and on the other seeks escape from that infernal cycle; for only the knowledge of absolute unity, of Being, brings liberation – *moksha* or *mukti* – literally the breaking of the ties of birth and of deeds. A figure still very much alive in modern India personifies what can only be called the inherent contradiction of Hinduism; everywhere, on the streets, at the doors of temples, one sees these *sadhus*, recognizable by the ochre garments they usually wear. Certain symbols distinguish them: for example, the Vishnuite will have a rosary of smooth little beads made of *tulasi* wood, while the Saivite will wear round his neck a rosary of thick rugged beads made of *rudraksha*. But these differences do not matter, for, in any case, the

modern *sadhu* undoubtedly combines in his own person many ancient religious figures: the Jainite Shraman, the Shivite Yoga, the Brahmanical Sannyasin, the Buddhist Bhikshu or beggar-monk. What matters is that he is a man who has renounced everything – his poverty, his family, his caste – to devote himself to meditation, to yoga, to asceticism according to his sect. It is he who will attain salvation, the ultimate truth, before anyone else, or rather, who has condemned all else in the name of this ultimate truth. His goal, whatever his way towards it, is to lose his own individuality and to merge with the Absolute which is all. Knowledge of the true can be reached only through the total destruction of empirical knowledge of the illusory. At the first stage, contact of a mystical kind, if no more than momentary, with supreme reality, will have made *maya* lose its power. Detachment from the world will result and lead, at any rate on the death of the 'knower', to his being lost in Unity. His individuality having disappeared even before death, his last acts will have left no mark and he will not be reborn. The philosophy of Sankara – this fundamental yearning for the Absolute which is beyond all determination, this negative theology, almost without a counterpart – can be lived only by the *sadhu*.

The marvel is that in this prodigious undertaking by the man himself to destroy what is human in him, in the name of an immanent Absolute, he goes on being. This spiritual outlook, it seems to me, is precisely an extension of the metaphysic implicit in the way the Hindu sinks into nature instead of making a stand against it to conquer it; on the religious plane, he no longer confines himself to being an element of everything, he identifies himself with everything by suppressing its parts.

But let us come down from these heights to consider the real marvel: here is a type of religious figure, the *sadhu*, who has no caste because he is beyond that, who has no further duties as a man because he has raised himself above mankind, who, in short, has voluntarily placed himself outside Hindu society, and all other human society, and who is accepted, more than that, fed, venerated and sustained by this rigid society of castes and *dharma*. He is the living negation of what has bred him; in a world where one is exhorted to increase and multiply, he is vowed to chastity; where one must give in return for every gift, he takes and gives

144

nothing; where prayers and ritual sacrifices must be offered, he assumes the place of the divinity to whom oblations are made. How often have I seen a *sadhu* allowed on to a station platform without a ticket, go into a temple where, without being asked his caste or religious sect, he is received with all the honours!

I know; our sociologists will at once pin a name on this phenomenon: the welcome accorded the *sadhu* is the safety-valve for a society constricted by observance of its laws; the vocation of the *sadhu* is the reaction to social pressures stronger here than anywhere else. Possibly, even probably, if you insist; but where does that get us? The safety-valve in this case threatens to blow everything up. Hindu society has been aware of that danger for a long time. It is not

unlikely that when these outlaws first appeared – always supposing that they were not already there – Brahmanical orthodoxy felt itself menaced, as ancient writings go to show. But as with everything else, it ended by accommodating itself in absorbing and institutionalizing the *sadhu*. It was ruled that every high-caste man must go through three or four stages according to the books, but the essential thing is that, after a period as a bachelor which corresponds to that of Brahmanical studies, a further stage when he is the head of a househould, married and the father of a family, he can – once his children have been reared and his wife's life is assured – renounce everything to become a hermit. That did the trick; Hindu society had ensured its perpetuation while safeguarding the salvation and the aspiration for non-rebirth of its members. It is probable that this law of the three stages of life has remained theoretical or is very rarely applied, but its spirit has profoundly affected the modern Hindu. I have never yet met an Indian of caste (thought there must be a handful) who has not proclaimed his faith in the ultimate unity of all beings. He humbly admits himself incapable of entering into a knowledge of unity in this life, but he believes in it on the evidence of the sacred writings and the experience of the great 'knowers.' The very few 'fulfilled' – *siddha* – are silent about the content of this experience, which is strictly ineffable; only the remarkable expression of their eyes, filled with strange light, bears witness that they have seen what no man has seen.

So at last we have come to that India which makes our apprentice-mystics of the West fall into ecstasy and raise their eyes to heaven. They turn away from their native culture to learn from yogis that one attains to the Absolute by sheer strength; a curious exaltation of human effort whose only aim is to destroy oneself.

But this is a mistake: the Hindu believes in and aspires to unity, believes that all religions combine insofar as they teach mankind that there is an Absolute and that 'ultimately they are one', according to the formula which constantly crops up. However, he makes no claim to live at the level of this intuition. It is, indeed, quite easy to understand this: if access to the Absolute means the destruction of the values here on earth and of the reality of the world, there are two very distinct planes with no communication between them: that of the world and everyday behaviour and that of the Absolute where nothing exists any longer but the one and peerless Brahma. There is no one in a hundred thousand who attains to the level of the ultimate; the Hindu masses thus remain on the same plane as the rest of humanity, neither higher nor lower.

The contradiction is therefore less between the Hinduism of caste and that of the Brahman. Theoretically they are incompatible and can only co-exist – peacefully. In fact a Hindu will be annoyed if you talk of contradiction; he will jump from one plane to the other to resolve the problems, until you on your side are annoyed by what appears to be a perpetual running-away from the argument.

Dare I go further and dismiss both those who can only see the contradiction in the duality of the planes of Hinduism and those who reconcile everything in Brahmanism? It must be acknowledged that most of those who claim to be 'monists,' or disciples of Sankara, have not read one word of the Master and invoke him at second or third hand. They would probably be very much taken aback if one revealed some of the exact points of his doctrine. But the unchallenged prestige of this scholar of the monist Vedanta is itself rather surprising; Sankara is by no means the only interpreter of sacred scriptures; and he is even, if one looks into it, amongst those who do their very best to make these writings conform with their own views. Innumerable philosophical-religious sects have challenged him and his insistence on absolute monism; they still go on doing so today and in theory number many adepts. So why the supremacy of Sankara? If one turns to Europe and to what is known of India there, one finds that Sankara is regarded as the only Indian philosopher, the one who represents the quintessence of Hindu thought. In this respect, as a matter of fact, our contemporaries are only following in the footsteps of the 19th-century Germans – Schopenhauer and Deussen – and there is good reason to believe that Westerners are partly responsible for Sankara's reputation. He has become, without anyone being aware of it, for the West no less than for the East, the representative of the final development of Hinduism. Yet for the Indians he is no more than the incarnation of Siva, which does not make them forget Krishna, the incarnation of Vishnu, who is the paramount deity of Hindu worship.

When I tell Indians that I am studying their philosophy, they ask me at once and without exception whether I have read the *Bhagavad-Gita*. They have all read and meditated upon it, they have all listened to lectures on it and studied commentaries on the *Gita* (other than that by Sankara). Far more often than the difficult commentaries of the great monist, or even of the Upanishads, this is the bedside-book of every Hindu, epitomizing his moral, mystical and doctrinal theology. It instructs him how to carry out his caste duties in a disinterested way, as we have seen, even if these duties consist of killing his brothers in war; it teaches him trust in God, in a divinity who, in certain aspects, is a personal divinity, to whom the devout man can address himself as to an individual, a divinity who loves him and has chosen him: 'Not by the Vedas, not by sacrifice, not by scripture-reading, nor yet by grim austerities can I be seen in such a form by any but thee in the world of men, O hero of the Kurus,' * says Krishna to Arjuna in the 11th hymn of the *Gita*, after having revealed himself to him as a cosmic totality. And this love of God for his votaries is referred to in other fundamental books of devotion such as the *Bhagavata Purana*. At the same time, and in the same texts, God appears as supremely impassive: 'All beings I regard alike; not one is hateful to me or beloved' **, and when he manifests himself to Arjuna in a mystical vision, he is none other than the cosmos itself. The God of Indian devotion – *bhakti* – who responds to the same eternal needs of the human heart as exist anywhere else, never detaches himself wholly from his immanence in the world. He is personal and endowed with feelings only in the eyes of popular piety; to thought he reveals himself both far beyond and within at the same time; the universe is his manifestation rather than his creation, he reveals it as much as he hides it, and each man is in himself in some sort a manifestation of God. Here, it seems to me, is a much more profoundly Hindu conception than Sankara's philosophy, certainly more widely held and not the prerogative of any one caste. Doubtless it is more popular because a representable, manifested God is more accessible than the extreme abstraction of the One. But it is also something quite different: the devotee of

---

* From 'The Bhagavad-Gita'. W. D. P. Hill. O.U.P. 1928.
** Ibid.

Vishnu, whether in the form of Krishna or any other, will also say that 'ultimately' God is beyond all distinctions, that his manifestation in the world is no more than a divine trick, not quite real. This, in fact, is what allows the Hindu to call God by every kind of name. But he refuses all the same to sacrifice the plural aspect of the deity to his unity. He does not cut off communication between the planes as the disciples of Sankara do; it is the Absolute itself which, on the one hand, manifests itself in the shape of the universe and on the other incarnated in a more precise way in this or that divine figure. Cosmic variety is the aspect which the fertility of the Absolute assumes, its desire to project itself into innumerable forms: 'The Being will desire to be many and to beget...' Says the *Chandoya Upanishad*, one of the oldest of the series, which bears witness to the antiquity of this world outlook.

The Hindu, therefore, has the strongest sense of the unity of everything, of the relativity of differences, but at the same time he immerses himself with delight in cosmic abundance. There is peculiar joy in the plurality of forms, in diversity for diversity's sake, as there is an ecstatic aspiration to unity, to merge with everything. He sees a connection between the one and the multiple which allows him, at will, to enjoy to the full the pleasures of life or give himself up to complete asceticism. There is a very beautiful iconographic symbol of this duality of outlook in the entwined figures of Siva and his Shakti: the Shakti, literally power but also potentiality, is the female aspect of the divinity, the fertile aspect through which he will deploy himself in the world of forms. The Shakti, who is thus plurality in power, holds Siva in a passionate embrace while he looks at her, completely impassive and immobile. But Siva himself symbolizes the dual movement of resorption and expansion of forms. The *Nataraja*, the king of the dance, is Siva dancing in the intoxication of the creation or destruction of worlds; while on the other hand the central figure of the Elephanta *Mahadeva* (Siva) is Siva withdrawn in the peace of un-differentiation.

This is the key to those shameful practices which are spoken of only in whispers and to which the name of tantrism is given. To most people tantrism is equivalent either to Black Magic – and it certainly includes it in Malabar, as amongst the Tibetan Buddhists – or to a sort of more

or less perverted sexual mysticism. People in general do
not know that the sexual practices are last in the scale of
tantrist initiation rites and that very, very few ever reach
them. Also, one should distinguish between those who may
indulge in these practices with their wives and those who
are sufficiently 'advanced' to indulge in them with any
woman; the latter are practically non-existent. In short,
the tantric method finds a place in the perspective that I
have just described, in the connection between the one
and the multiple; it is the spiritual path which claims to
lead man towards the undifferentiated Absolute by the exaltation and complete control over natural powers and vital
functions; the sexual function, being the most difficult to
control in practice, is introduced at the last stage of the
road towards identification with the Absolute. It marks the
disappearance of all human emotions, the final appeasement
of the vital.

But our key is in fact a genuine master-key. We can
use it to enter into an understanding of many aspects of
Indian culture, and to a rather more discriminating judgment
of what, at first glance, tends to repel us.

Images

Is the Hindu an idolator? The question seems absurd
because, in all probability, idolatry has never existed. A
statue represents a deity or a saint; it is neither the deity
nor the saint. It is a help, a sort of material support for
the prayers of the devout; it comes to the aid of the faltering
imagination. If the use of images had been idolatrous, Ig-
natius Loyola and his Exercises would be the veritable
archetype of idolators.

This argument applies to the Hindu, *mutatis mutandis*.
He, who believes in the ultimate unity of all things, could
not see in the statue of the Krishna child or the flute-playing
shepherd the God himself, who defies any form of representation, since he is none of his manifestations. And yet the
question arises: is the Hindu an idolator? Or, rather, one
should say, is the Indian? For it is not only Krishna's worshippers who decorate his statue, coax it, implore it as
though it were Krishna himself. The Christian in Indian

churches needs statues, not only to kneel before them, but also to caress and embrace them (though this is hardly less common in Southern European countries, after all). In the Catholic churches, there is a statue for pretty well every saint in the calendar. One corner of the church is reserved to display the day's statue. St. Anthony of Padua claims his eight days, but there are also St. Sebastian and all the rest. When the statue of the Virgin is quite new and white and in her gaudiest attire, the parish priest puts her under glass to protect her from the fervour of the pious, who then come and stroke the glass.

But none of this would have presented a problem to me: there are extravagant feelings of piety which have to find some mode of expression, and why not this one? However, I altered my opinion when a man who repaired statues – Hindu statues this time – told me one day he had had to give up doing repairs in the home. He would be sent for to replace the arm of a Krishna or some Devi – for a mutilated image cannot be used in worship – but as soon as he started nailing he was always stopped by one of more of the women, who sobbed: 'No, no, you mustn't do that, you'll hurt him!' After various experiences of this kind he insisted on taking the gods away for repair in order to be able to hammer away in peace.

Have we any proof of Hindu idolatry? None; and we shall never have it; the God always remains something beyond his images, but it is at the same time true that a statue has a quite different connotation here from that amongst Christians in our countries. It is taken as an exact reproduction of one of the manifestations chosen by the deity through which he makes himself known to men. It is more than a reproduction, it is a commemoration, the perpetuated presence of that manifestation; something like a sacrament, like the authentic but veiled reality of the divinity accorded to his worshippers. This is no doubt the reason why painting, which saw such great development in Buddhist India – as Ajanta and Bagh, and also Sigiriya in central Ceylon, bear witness – later disappeared or at any rate was superseded by architecture and, above all, by sculpture. I know that frescoes have been discovered in the sanctuary of the great temple of Tanjore; the oldest temples of Kanchipuram bear the remains of paintings; but there is nothing comparable in breadth, even if the art is the same, to that produced during the Buddhist period. In fact the Hindu is not satisfied with the two-dimensional image of the deity; he needs a plastic expression, with the three dimensions of real bodies, something tangible, an abode made ready for divinity. It was not until Mughal influence made itself felt that Rajput painting developed and turned to religious subjects.

That is also why the 'sight' – *darshan* – of the God's statue is the most important moment of the visit to a temple. To offer a sacrifice is nothing, one must also have been in the presence of the God if only for an instant. There is no other explanation for the rush of worshippers to the Kali at Khaligat, to the Vithoba (Krishna) at Pandharpur. The *sadhu*, it could be said, is no more than another of these manifestations of the divine – or of the deity, it makes no difference – the essential thing is that the inaccessible is made accessible, which accounts for the welcome which he is accorded by everyone and the importance of *darshan*. Every famous *sadhu*, whom many people claim as their *guru*, has to show himself daily to his disciples, and even strangers come to see him for no particular reason. There is no need to make conversation; the sight of the saint is enough, a fulfilment in itself. Gandhi, too, who was revered as a *guru* during his lifetime and before he became an incarnation of Vishnu, had to lend himself to the ceremony of *darshan* wherever he went.

The divine, being nowhere, is also everywhere. Everything is a manifestation of it and, above all, whatever explicitly brings it back to people's memory. The interplay of the one and the plural seems in this respect to work in favour of the plural, but the one is not overlooked; it remains in the background, it lies at the end of efforts which will never be made to identify oneself with it. Then there will be no further need for statues; the divine can as easily dwell within formless stone; and one finds such by the thousand in the Indian countryside, at the foot of trees, on the banks of rivers, with or without a place of worship built around them. One might be tempted to think that these stones, blackened by sacrificial oil, reddened by *kumkum* powder, are more able to represent the No-form than the too human outlines of classical sculpture. Their prototype would then be the cylindrical stone – the *linga* – the ancient phallic symbol which represents Siva, the starkest image of divinity. Placed in the dark sanctuary of a temple, it brings the faithful almost directly into the presence of an ineffable Absolute which infinitely surpasses their human conceptions. This is a far cry from the still very sentimental worship of Krishna.

There is thus a duality in the representation of the divine which in some way stands for the two poles of its conception. I should like an expert to try and trace it too in the various styles of the temples; by and large, though they may be dynastic or regional, they nevertheless show a deep unity of conception, or rather a profound duality which distinguishes the inspiration of the North from that of the South. The northern style is spread over a sort of arc from Badama, on the western border of the Deccan, to Konarak in Orissa on the east coast, passing through Khajuraho, where it finds its culmination. Without going into technical details, the northern style seems to me to be distinguished at first sight by a multiplicity of architectural ornamentation; one's eyes do not soar straight up to the

Bhuvaneshvar in the North

top of the *sikhara* which symbolises the mystical heights to be attained. There are projections, recessions, protuberances on the side of the *sikhara*. The outline of the whole seems a trifle mannered and precious. Further, the profusion of reliefs and statues arrests the eye, transforming the stone fabric into a living pyramid; aspiring to the summit, the onlooker pauses with enjoyment and may even lose sight of the end. Here the unity of all does not militate against plurality. The exaltation of forms, and of very beautiful, very human and often very sensuous forms, does not in any way make one forget the ultimate No-form; this is something like the tantric ideal translated into stone, and something, indeed which corresponds to a contemporary flowering of tantrism.

To compare this style with that of the South is rather like comparing a Mozart sonata to a Haydn one. The style is known generally as Indo-Aryan, to distinguish it from that of the tip of the peninsula, which is Dravidian. These names seem to me pretty inept; if Southern art is Dravidian,

Tanjore in the South

then Sankara philosophy is purely Dravidian and not All-Indian. In fact, in the great temple of Tanjore, built under the Cholas somewhere about the year 1000, and which represents the peak of Southern art, there are no more of these flourishes and graces to enjoy and linger over. Eyes and spirit are lifted upwards to the summit of the pyramidal roof which surmounts the sanctuary. This contains a *linga*, as little titillating to the imagination as the very pure lines of the building. There are few sculptures, and those few have a rather austere aspect. Everything is sacrificed to the unity of the whole, to the ascent towards the summit, as with Sankara. When one leaves Tanjore – or, for that matter, Gangeikondacholapuram – for Khajuraho or Bhuvaneshvar, it is as though one were skipping many centuries, passing from early Gothic to baroque. The extraordinary thing is that this is not at all the case: they are contemporaneous and technically equal, thus synchronizing the two extremes of Hindu spirituality (while true Indian 'baroque' is to be found at Vijayanagar).

So it is not surprising that the temple should be the privileged abode, as the statue is the presence, of the deity. Although the Hindu is not obliged to go to the temple, he does go very often, having put himself in a state of ritual purity on each occasion. By its very structure, and by the worship which takes place there, the temple points the spiritual way to the faithful.

I do not think I am far wrong in interpreting in the same way the triumphal welcome accorded to the statue of Our Lady of Fatima in Southern India a few years ago. Hindus and Muslims were by no means the slowest to decorate the streets through which she passed. Muslims – I might say devotees of iconoclastic Islam – were most anxious to receive her; Fatima, Fatma – was she not perhaps the daughter of the Prophet? For everyone she represented no less than a sacrament, and a miracle was expected of her.

But the most revered and classical temples contain very much more than statues of gods and goddesses, very much else besides reliefs on epico-religious subjects. In all ages the pillars and even the walls have furnished artists with surfaces to decorate where their imagination could have full rein. Does one not see in the romanesque churches of Europe chapels covered with monsters who bear not the slightest relation to revealed scripture; *'Hi sunt elephantes'*, remarks one of them, to make quite sure that there shall be no misunderstanding. The Indian pillars and walls of Ellora in Madura present a mass of leafage, of stylized lotuses, of opposed animals, such as that oft-repeated motif of two beasts with one head, on this side an elephant, on that a bull. Perhaps the temples of Hoysala in Belus (12th century) and Halebid (13th) have the finest examples of animal and plant friezes.

These fantasies, though wholly profane, do not shock you. But it is rather different when you come upon the representation of human forms in the niches ornamented with graceful contorted silhouettes, as at Khajuraho or

Durga Temple

Bhuvaneshvar, or even on the Kailasha of Ellora where demi-gods frame more important deities, in the dissertation on the dance unfolded in stone at Chidambaram, or finally in the full dissertation on love as in the sun temple of Konarak, where all forms of love play are depicted, one after the other. Erotic motifs are not by any means peculiar to Konarak, they are in fact one of the constant features of temple decoration and, in the South, of the heavy processio-

nal teakwood chariots. They are even to be found on the
pillars of the Mount-Abu Jainist temples in an exceedingly
puritanical religious context, at Khajuraho, amongst the
Vishnuites of Srirangam and the Saivites of Madura, though
they are never of great antiquity. Before these artlessly or
skilfully erotic scenes, surprise ranges from hearty laughter
to virtuous indignation. One is even more indignant when
the guide draws attention to them without so much as thinking of giving them a mystical interpretation.

Can fantasy really go as far as that? Is eroticism to be
laid bare even in the temples? So many profane matters
to catch the eyes of worshippers? That is precisely the
point; is there anything that is absolutely profane to the
Hindu or, to put it another way, anything which is not
part of religion? I have already referred to the representation
of Siva and his Shakti as a human couple embracing. The
ecstasy of love appears to be the best approach to supreme
happiness; it is not yet total identification with the Absolute,
but the joy of the awakening has a higher consciousness; it
is the universe which, in all its multiplicity, clasps the unity
from which it proceeds. I will not go so far as to say that
all the sports of love depicted in the stones of Konarak
and Khajuraho are also symbols of this unity-plurality.
No; they are what they are and nothing more; but the act
of love, in itself, means to the Hindu penetrating the sacred;
it is not something set apart, something slightly guilty. There
is no spark of puritanism in him; all nature is religious.
He, too, has discovered that the sexual act has a double
end, immediate satisfaction and procreation, and he refuses
to exalt the one in order to denigrate the other. Without
being a deliberate symbol of a higher reality, human love,
in its physical aspect, symbolizes the act whereby the deity
creates the world and the pleasure he derives from it.

The very human figures which decorate the recesses
and bare surfaces are probably also in no way out of place
in the Hindu's eyes; there are even gigantic couples which
stand out against the façade of Karla. At first sight this
profusion of human shapes seems to contradict the lowly
place man occupies in the universe and, more particularly,
the fact that he has no ultimate reality: the Karla caves
are Buddhist, as a matter of fact, which does not leave
any doubt whatever about the underlying metaphysic.
Nevertheless, man is, in the scale of terrestial beings, the

one most capable of raising himself to final liberation. Vishnu could be incarnated in a boar, a turtle, a fish, but he was still and first of all Vishnu; man remains, particularly if he is of high caste, the nearest to true knowledge. The deity whom the pious worship has a marked preference for taking on human form: it is in this guise that he makes himself known to those who adore him, and the vision of the universe identified with Krishna, the Krishna-universe, in the eleventh poem of the *Bhagavad-Gita,* remains a rare experience, one which would overwhelm the common run of mankind. So the Vishnuite religion devotes special worship to the incarnation of its God in human form: there are countless temples to Krishna. Rama, too, has his devotees, particularly at Ayodhya, his place of origin, while other avatars of Vishnu, though represented, are not the object of a special cult. The needs of the religious spirit are everywhere the same: if it has not the power to rise to the heights of absolute unity, it requires a deity in which it can recognize itself, which it can love. And precisely because man is able to aspire to the Absolute, he himself has something of the divine, even in his outward appearance. This is probably what a very ancient treatise on painting, the *Citralakshana,* means when it says that men should be depicted with the expression of those who seek peace – *shanti.* The peace referred to here is obviously ultimate peace, the peace which come of knowledge and of final fusion with the Absolute.

It is within this framework again that one must see what I shall call the hero-worship accorded in India to anyone who has risen at all above the common rut. No country has so many memorials, inscriptions to the memory of so-and-so, steles and monuments to great men. Since cremation is the rule, the Hindu does not have tombs where he can commemorate the dead, but he has amply compensated for them. In about 1950 I was amazed to find in every house I entered a sort of shrine with the portraits of the five great architects of Indian independence: Gandhi, of course; and Nehru; Rajendra Prasad, President of India; C. Rajagopalachari; and Netaji Subhas Chandra Bose, the Indian Nazi who, during the war, raised a militia to fight for Hitler and Japan. The different political shades, the nature of the services rendered by each of these men were of no account; it was enough that their names had been

Stalin fan?

associated, in one way or another, with the struggle for independence. But that is not all. It is in India that I have frequently, almost constantly, heard Hitler's praises sung; Germans are congratulated on being his compatriots. One tries to find a rational explanation for this attitude: Hitler, like India, was fighting Britain. That was roughly Subhas Chandra Bose's reasoning. But it would be quite wrong to attribute it to the mass of Hitler's admirers. Nor is the reason that Indians cherish an innate liking for totalitarianism; I am more inclined to think they have no very clear idea of what it means. No, the Führer was, quite simply, 'a great historical force,' as someone said to me, 'a natural force', as another put it. In a context where the individual himself is nothing, grandiosity of ideas, or of evil, can only be evidence of powerful cosmic forces far beyond the individual who, by that token, is nearer than anyone else to the divine, in closer communion with the design of the universe, a more precise manifestation of the Absolute in action in the world. Since, in any case, the plane of phenomena and of history has no ultimate reality other than the unity which constitutes them, the sufferings and evils of this world are only relative; they outrage people's feelings very little, or not at all. The Indian does not see tragedy in his own history; how should he see it in the history of others?

Hero-worship does take the form of monuments, but portraits are good enough, so long as they can be hung with garlands on anniversaries and other occasions. Indispensable to this cult, however, are unquestionably speeches. The word comes naturally here. People can improvise a speech lasting an hour and a half (at least) with the greatest of ease and go on repeating platitudes for the thousandth time with the most inspired manner and a truly Asiatic eloquence. The orator is carried along by his audience. The Indian crowd listens and seems never to tire of listening; indeed, it is always a little disappointed by Nehru's appearances since, in the brevity of his orations, he is an exception to the rule. No commemoration of any kind can take place without four or five speeches from specially invited guests, not counting the introductory speech, the concluding remarks, and the vote of thanks. As a foreigner one soon gets to know this and stops attending these functions; but the Indian is a rewarding audience; he will go again and again to listen tirelessly to lectures which are not only interminable but all exactly alike; and afterwards he will earnestly discuss whether Dr. So-and-so 'spoke well'. The great men being celebrated are rather overlooked in all this; the main thing is that, lulled by the stream of words, one feels for a moment lifted above oneself, carried on the vast tide of cosmic unity, embarked in a vessel out of one's control. The sound waves beat rhythmically against the listener's ear, and he responds more to the physical vibration than to the sense of the words. He does not fall asleep, no; he is only in a state of quietude from which he has no wish to emerge.

Let us hold on to our key; it should open further doors to us.

Music and dancing, it seems, are the most favoured subjects for temple friezes. Apart from the *Natyasastra* (Dissertation on the Dance) which is unfolded on the base of the Hall of a Thousand Columns at Chidambaram, apart from the more profane reliefs which delightfully run round the huge plinth known as the 'King's Throne' at Vijayanagar, there are thousands of representations of dancers and musicians on the pillars and friezes of temples. Our classical culture can be of some use to us here for a moment: as in Greece, music and dance are essentially religious in origin; they play the same part that they played for us in the Mysteries of the Middle Ages. Perhaps more effective teaching than that engraved on stone, music and dancing combine to bring to life for the Hindu this or that episode from the *Ramayana* or the *Mahabharata*. Until recent years performances were staged in the temples themselves, just as the early Mysteries were performed inside our churches. The *devadasi,* or servants of God, were the performers. Even today, although they have shifted from the temple to the theatre (often open to the sky), Hindu music and dancing are almost entirely religious. The best proof of this, perhaps, is that even in folk songs religious inspiration plays a great part. It is indeed in song that Hindu religious devotion expresses itself traditionally, and one must have been present in one or other of the Vishnuite temples at those long sessions of *bhajan,* where hands clap out the rhythm, to understand what the essence of music and rhythm means to the Hindu. All the devotional poems, those of Kabir like those of Tukaram, are designed to be chanted in chorus in this way. The melody is less important than the rhythm: after all, the song must lend itself to the tread of pilgrims on the march as well as to the beat of the drum.

But I wonder whether music – and dancing when it accompanies it – is not something more than one means of religious expression. It has sometimes seemed to me that for the Hindu it is the only true language of religion. Of course, this music is always vocal – the drum and the cymbals are only there to mark the rhythm – so one ought really

to say that *song* is the only true language of religion. I shall venture for once to emerge from the purely Hindu atmosphere and illustrate what I mean by an example taken from an aboriginal tribe living at the southernmost point of the Western Ghats, quite close to Cape Comorin. This will perhaps allow me to repair a little the injustice I have done, of which I am only too well aware: once you postulate that the aboriginal tribes as a whole are alien to Hinduism, you tend to overlook them completely and not to perceive that they have derived a great deal from Hindu culture and vice versa. Thus, in these Kanikkaran villages, in deep forests and at an altitude of some 3,300 feet, where nothing is known of caste, I was intensely surprised when, on my first visit, the dense crowd of aborigines who would not move an inch away from me (this being their first sight of a white woman) scattered the moment I was brought something to eat. Here, too, food is amongst prohibited objects, to the extent that mealtimes were the only moments of privacy I had. Even at night, in the small lattice-work cabin where I was supposed to retire, I remained under the benevolent supervision of numerous pairs of eyes.

One evening, while with these same Kanikkarans, when I and the ethnologist friend I had come with had the honour of being entertained by the chief sorcerer of the tribe, the elders of the village gathered round us. We talked by the flickering light of an oil-lamp and in the smoke of *bidis* (little local cigarettes rolled in tobacco-leaf instead of paper). We knew by then that every village in the tribe had its own or more than one guardian spirit; but we wanted to know the history of the tutelary spirit of the village we were in. The elders looked at each other uncomfortably, and finally one of them said, 'we couldn't *tell* you the history, but we can *sing* it.' Straight away someone went off to fetch two drums and a man began to sing, or rather to intone a sort of recitative, the drums marking the beat. The fact is that we shall never know anything of that history, for the language of the recitative is not that used in conversation. Is it a religious language, peculiar to this type of song? Or is it the original tribal language, now discarded in favour of the language of the surrounding plains? We shall never know that either. But our companions obviously understood the song which remained a closed book to us.

What is the peculiar virtue of music and rhythm, of this

monotonous recitative? It was the same tribe that provided the answer. It was not long after the voice had risen and the drums had begun to sound that one of the musicians, his fingers still playing automatically on the drum, threw back his head, showing the whites of his eyes. No one was in the least startled by the trance which had carried the man far from the hut where we were all gathered; on the contrary, they respected it, and waited for it to come to an end, together with the throbbing rhythms of the instruments. Later the ecstatic would have to be taken to a distant sanctuary to appease the goddess whose domain he had thus involuntarily violated.

It is the same in Hindu society; but this experience, cursed among the Kanikkarans, is, on the contrary, sought after by the Hindus, who prize it highly. It is one of the highest moments of communion with the Absolute, arrived at by losing awareness of self, and it is come by through music, or through a combination of music and dancing.

Of the various kinds of dancing which one finds in India only that of Manipur seems to be purely plastic without any symbolic meaning, though I would hesitate to assert this too categorically. The others all claim to be telling a story and to be teaching something by the pose, the rhythm, and the song associated with them. From this one might think that these dances are purely on the plane of the multiple, like the temple statues and the worship of a god in human form. Is not the ineffable, by definition, that which cannot be represented? The richness of the costumes, the extraordinary variety of gestures and of their significance, which brings into play not only the arms and legs, but the face, the eyes, and neck, all carry us into a legendary world of heroes and gods, and not into that of Brahman; the songs themselves, whose mode varies according to what they are trying to express, appeal more to the psychological than to the spiritual. And yet, if you have the opportunity to watch not one of those performances given today in India – as abroad – by the great artists for audiences seeking entertainment, but one of those religious occasions where the crowd comes to meditate as at a liturgy, you have to change your mind. The length of the performance, the myriad scintillations of jewels and brocades under the floodlights, the uninterrupted beating of the drums, the ornamentation of the melody round the dominant, everything tends towards a single end which the Westerner would define in one word: stupefaction. But the Hindu sees something quite different in it. He goes to the concert or the dance to escape – from time that flies, from the confines of self and his own psyche. But, you will say, we're also looking for something of the sort when we go to a concert or a ballet. No, I do not think so. Or, at any rate, if the experience does have something analogous, it is differently formulated. There is nothing, or practically nothing, aesthetic in the Hindu's ecstasy, or perhaps one should say, the aesthetic and the religious are absolutely indistinguishable from one another. In our case, the individual submerges himself in a work of art; the Hindu loses himself too, but primarily to commune with a limitless Absolute beyond the rhythm and the melody. He rediscovers unity – once again – through a very special plurality; it is no doubt the same rhythm indefinitely repeated which suggests eternity, the same prolonged glitter of light which makes him lose consciousness of physical light and gives him access to light invisible. If catharsis through art has ever existed, it is certainly here that it takes place. The religious essence of art cannot itself be properly understood except in this context of the total immanence of the divine, wherein it succeeds in leaving the boundaries of individual consciousness to reunite with an absolute beyond time and space.

The greatest luck for the foreigner visiting India would be to be able to attend a Kathakali festival for a whole week in the south of the Malabar Coast. The Kathakali is peculiar to that region. As with so many other aspects of Kerala culture, some people attribute to Chinese influence the use of special masks and of a curtain held and waved behind the dancers, even before the performance starts, and also the character of mimed and sung drama of the Kathakali. It does not really matter whether these features are or are not derived from the Far East. One thing is certain: the Kathakali is profoundly Hindu and could not be anything but Hindu, like so many other things borrowed and assimilated by India.

In the past, each performance lasted at least a whole night. Today it does not take much more than four hours. This alone shows us the Indian's capacity for concentrated attention – we who are exhausted by a concert lasting two hours. But if we turn up at the start, when the 'atmosphere'

Kathakali

of the play is being created, we shall certainly have had almost enough by the time the curtain falls (that is, when it is raised). On the edge of the stage, between the actors and the audience, the wicks of a large oil lamp are lit, the intermingling flames of which remind one of the worship of the Jamna at Mathura. That is the only light throughout the performance. From time to time more oil is poured in and the flame leaps up a little higher, causing greater strain on the eyes. The stage is thus filled with dancing shadows which contribute to the animation of the dancers' movements (or actors': it is difficult to know which to call them). A good half hour before the beginning of the performance the drum starts to beat time. When the curtain begins to shake at last – the real prelude to the entry of the characters on the stage – one is well primed; dazed and blinded, one is already in close communion with the stage before anything has taken place. I have made it a practice to attend this preparation of minds and bodies, believing that it was necessary to an understanding of the whole. On one occasion however, I failed to do so in order to see things from behind the scenes. The preparation of the actors is even more drawn-out than that of the public. The make-up is elaborate and requires very expert assistants. The actors have to lie, sit and turn in every direction. But each one is absorbed in his task, and silence prevails throughout. There is nothing hectic, nothing hasty; all movements are very deliberate, and when one of the players is ready to go on you see him collect himself and pause for a moment, with his hands raised in the *anjali*. I cannot put into words the astonishing impression of depersonalization which these men give. They are not concerned with themselves or with the effect they are going to produce. You cannot even say that they are already in the skins of their characters; for these are for-

malized and expressed by the mask, the gestures, the leaps, the very stylized cries which depict the character without the actor putting in anything of his own; his words are sung by other actors in the wings. No, the actor seems more as though endowed with a higher mission, charged to transmit a message infinitely beyond his own person.

As for the performance itself – often an episode from the *Ramayana* – I am incapable of describing it. I do not know whether it is beautiful or ugly. I know only that one is caught up as in a net by a sort of sympathetic magic which only ceases with the drum, the singing and the great flame of the lamp. The Hindus come away from it as from the temple; the week-long festival is an annual retreat for them. They do not have the idea, confronted again by the exploits of their divine heroes, that they have to 'rethink' their Hindu faith; it is enough that for a week they should have lived more intensely in communion with the universe and with its unity through the enchantment of the Kathakali.

Ahimsa

But the Hindu has a means of being in permanent communion with the sacrament of the universe: for centuries he has made a vow of peace to all creatures. Some believe that non-violence was invented by Gandhi. Certainly it was he who made it known to the world and turned it into a political weapon. But it would be very hard to date its first appearance in India. It cannot be a Vedic conception, for it is contradicted by the practice of animal sacrifice; this, indeed, may perhaps be one of the reasons why, very early, the Vedic religion, as such, fell into desuetude. Today when, for once in a way, a great sacrifice of this kind takes place, the chosen animals are led to the place of sacrifice but are not put to death, which seems nonsense in the context of Vedic ritual. *Ahimsa* (non-violence) is more likely to be contemporary with the Upanishadic revolution, with Buddhism and with Jainism, which is its strictest theorist. Even today religious Jainists do not go about without a little broom to sweep their paths for fear of crushing living things as they walk; they wear linen guards over their mouths when they speak in case they should swallow an insect by accident. Should they not, above all, avoid any contact with modern science? They are already allowed so few foods; if they came to know that everything was infested with microscopic living organisms, that plants are as much alive as animals, there would be nothing left for them to eat; they would scarcely be permitted to live. No doubt *ahimsa* was adopted by the Brahmans – like so many other things – even though it derived from other than brahmanical circles; in any case it has never won the support of the whole of India, and if in the end the high castes became its most fervent ad-

Jainist Monks

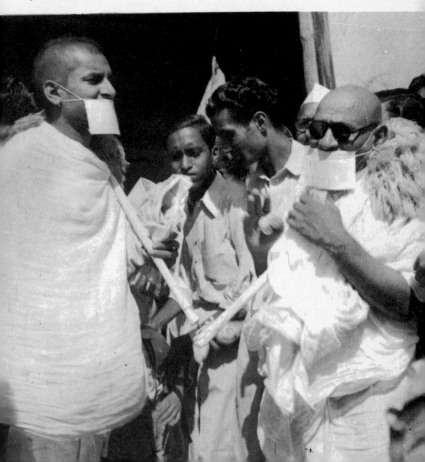

herents, there are still many people of low caste who are not, vegetarianism being one of the essential features of *ahimsa* for the Hindu. The Bengali Brahmans eat meat and fish; those in the Darbhanga region, formerly Mithila, must eat fish; it is one of their strict caste duties. One single form of meat is forbidden in the whole of India, and that is beef. How exactly the cow acquired sacred characteristics it is very difficult to establish. All that is known is that from the earliest times the cow was the emblem of all wealth, a symbol of abundance and of gratified desire. Is this enough to explain its time-honoured sacredness?

Even if we do not know exactly why the cow, of all animals, has achieved this elevated position, the solicitude of which she is the object is full of lessons on non-violence. In every village and small town only the most wretched household does not keep a cow. Lack of a cow would mean that no milk was drunk there, but also it would be a sign that one was bereft of all the blessings which the cow confers. When she is ill, she is not killed; if she is infirm, she is looked after, or else driven to a temple where the devout take responsibility for feeding her. If she has a calf it is never killed; it is reared, or allegedly reared. In actual fact, calves are condemned to death by the thousand from inanition since, as in our countries, people want to have the benefit of the cow's milk and do so without bothering about the calf. How often one sees an emaciated calf trailing miserably behind its mother, who is being taken to the customer to be milked (a very wise precaution on the customer's part, given the strong propensity to 'baptize' the milk). The cow makes difficulties about being milked as it is, so the calf is allowed to trail on as long as it lives; after its death, people even go so far as to make a dummy to encourage the cow. It is true that sometimes the cows themselves are quite appallingly thin. The Indian is in no good position to nourish his livestock, in particular his horned cattle, with his sparse and seasonal grass. Once I was sworn at when, mounted on an ox-cart which I had hired, I dared to throw away the skins of the bananas I was eating instead of giving them to the animals drawing me. Probably lack of nourishment is the most common form of death for these animals in any case. The leather industry, since there are no butchers, accounts for a certain number of cattle, and there has to be some way or other of killing

Birds' Hospital at Del

them in a country where public opinion will not, so far, tolerate slaughterhouses.

As for draught cattle, those used for tilling and for transporting loads or people, their owners try to feed them as best they can, but they are subjected to another type of torture; kicks and blows are unsparing. They are not, if it comes to that, the only ones to receive this treatment; there is not a cat, dog, or goat which does not automatically give human beings a wide berth, so accustomed are they to being hit and stoned. One could almost say that this is an Indian's instinctive reaction: the sight of a dog makes him pick up a stone, for no other reason than that it is a dog. It is true that the poor animal is regarded as unclean and that the Brahman has practically no other way of avoiding contact with it than to drive it off with a stone. But the cow and the dog share blows equally, and it may be thought that the question of cleanness and uncleanness has very little to do with the matter.

I do not think that India has ever had any theory about animals as machines; so it must be that their susceptibilities do not function like ours in this matter, and no *ahimsa* in the world will change it. One has to see both sides of the matter to try and understand it. The attitude of non-violence has never signified anything but respect for life as such; not respect for feelings, conscience, or personality. It is another one of those innumerable manifestations of the visceral beliefs of the Indian in the unity of everything and, in particular, the unity of life. Its only commandment is: thou shalt not kill. Life is the thing in which the dynamism of the Divine is made most manifest, in which it remains dynamic instead of becoming static as in a mineral or even a plant.

This is perhaps what explains why so many cruel legends have survived to nourish popular piety. The divine guest, in disguise, comes to a couple and asks them to kill their child and give it to him to eat. The Hindu glories in this legend, which occurs in endless variations, proving the power of the god, since he will bring the child to life again once he has tested the piety of the parents. The story is compared to that of the sacrifice of Isaac exacted by God of Abraham, an incident which upsets our feelings quite enough as it is, but the Hindu sees no difference at all between the consummated killing of his legend and the stayed

sacrifice of Genesis. When we try to show him the difference he retorts at once: didn't Abraham substitute an animal for his son and complete the sacrifice? He will always repudiate the idea that man has a special destiny; man is creature like any other and, indeed, there is often little difference between the way the Hindu treats a dog and his attitude towards his inferiors.

It was to this same *ahimsa* that Gandhi appealed. One of the main weapons of non-violence is the fast, which he used, as so many other Indians use it today, in furtherance of the most diverse aims. In recent years people have fasted to get the State frontiers they wanted – one *sadhu* died of starvation – and to get higher wages, and it is an effective form of strike action here. The Mahatma, as is known, fasted as often – if not more often – to expert pressure on his compatriots as on the British. I have always been surprised that Westerners accept the classification of fasting amongst non-violent weapons; it must be because they have never seen it in action and because its effectiveness is judged in advance as nil in our parts of the world. But have a look at it from here; there is no more terrible war of nerves, there is nothing like it to drive the crowd to the verge of riot. Hour by hour people enquire after the fasting man's condition, ask whether he is in danger. The pressure thus exercised on those against whom the fast is aimed can scarcely be called 'moral'. Even if the object of the fast is a bad one – and there is no guarantee that it should not be – there is such a large element of blackmail surrounding the person in danger of dying, the tension round him mounts so high, that one has to give way under what is pure co-ercion. Usually it is not so much the life of the fasting man as the hubbub created around him that wins the victory. Not only is the fast itself a weapon of violence, but it unleashes violence, and the same could be said of everything included – apart from the fast – in the tactics of the *satya-graha* (a policy of non-violence), including civil disobedience. Gandhi had to give up the collective *satyagraha,* a source of violence against the British, and in the end reserved it to himself. A few years ago Nehru similarly had to forbid the *satyagraha* aimed at Goa, and for the same reason: it was degenerating into violence. Gandhi was right in saying that the masses were not ready for the *satyagraha.* But could any crowd of human beings, as distinct from angels, ever be ready for it? In any case, it is an odd sort of non-violence, the idea of which could spring only from the Indian mind and in a context where little value is attached to human sensibility – which exists as much in India as anywhere else.

The Indian is very hospitable. It is not I who say so; it is he who proclaims it. He says that he is less hospitable in relation to his compatriots – is this owing to caste? – than to the *mleccha*, the foreigner, the complete stranger. Far be it from me to criticize Indian hospitality from which I have so greatly benefited. But to state the case precisely: in principle, the Indian has a truly Oriental sense of hospitality. The guest is respected and revered as a messenger from the gods, particularly the passing traveller who seems to have dropped from heaven. To the head of the house he presents an opportunity for discharging his duty of giving. The guest is like the *sadhu* in that he is not part and parcel of normal society but brings down blessings on those who make him welcome. In countless small ways one is aware that the attentions shown the guest are not directed entirely to his own person, but to something else, perhaps quite simply to *dharma*. I have so often heard people who invited me to visit them say: 'It's my duty to receive you', or: 'It's my duty to offer you a meal'.

That having been said, in practice one comes across wide differences. There are very poor villages who know nothing other than their poverty where the stranger is received with open arms and, though the people have nothing to offer, they nevertheless find something; they send to the village tea-shop for a mug of tea with-milk; and how many of these little tea-sellers themselves, under whose porches I have taken shelter from the monsoon rain, have offered me their tea without accepting payment. Then there are also the poor who know a bit too much about the rest of humanity and have become self-conscious. One has to establish one's credentials over a long period before being admitted to their homes. At the other extreme there are snobs who collect foreigners as other people collect stamps. The tourist may never get to know any but these, and more's the pity.

But there is a dark side to every picture; the day when I had to give up waiting for the post-office clerk who had disappeared I had talked of making a complaint to the Postmaster. The following day I received a visit from the clerk thus menaced. He came to my house to ask me – without a shadow of contrition – to withdraw my complaint, or rather my threat to complain; he was a poor man, the father of a family, and I would get him the sack. But that was not his main argument – for it is no use appealing to people's better feelings – no, he had come to see me in my home because I could not refuse to listen to a guest; the laws of hospitality would forbid it. That was unanswerable.

This is the India which, under the pacific – and no longer pacifist – aegis of Nehru, daily renews its declaration of peace to the world of men. It sees this as its special role, its historic mission; when one casts an eye over its past, its dynastic battles, its wars of conquest, one cannot help doubting this. And yet it is quite true that the India of today does try to maintain an equal distance between the two great power blocs. There are undoubtedly very clearly-defined political reasons for this, but that does not mean that it is being hypocritical in declaring its non-violence on the international plane. The error lies rather in interpreting this as a manifestation of a deeper and more sensitive humanity than that of ordinary mortals. It is a question of transposing – though in a rather vague way, one must admit – metaphysical belief into the domain of politics, and it is not so much concerned with mankind as with a certain conception of universal unity. *

---

* That is why, incidentally, there is no point in making a too precise intellectual analysis of this will to universal peace. I am thinking, for example, of the declaration of the *Panchashila* (the Five Principles) by Nehru and Chou En-lai, which repudiates any intervention in the internal affairs of neighbouring countries. The great champion of Asian nationalism could only associate himself with Chou En-lai by overlooking the invasion of Tibet by China, and the situation in the latter half of 1959 is fraught with dangers running counter to the Principles. Every Indian will tell you that Tibet is a Chinese province, which is equivalent to saying that Poland is a Russian province. It is only some of the Tibetans who unfortunately do not agree with this view.

Namaskar

'MAY I TAKE LEAVE?' I should like to slip away, in the Indian manner, after having asked permission in this curious form, for I have the feeling that my India is not quite that seen by the Indians, nor yet by those in love with the Absolute. But I have travelled this distance only to ask one question, a question about India which takes in far more than India itself.

We have seen that caste is condemned to die, at any rate in the long run, by progressive urbanization, and that is why I have stressed those elements in Hinduism which are not on the level of caste, the elements which one usually refers to as Hindu spirituality. It does seem as though, owing to the gulf between the mystique of reincarnation and the pursuit of salvation, the latter may survive in its present form when caste has disappeared.

That is the general sense of the hopes one hears expressed everywhere today: that there will be an eternal aspect of the Arab world, of China, and of India. Each of these groupings of mankind is adopting with greater or lesser speed the Western type of economic life, the social structures which are more and more determined by it and therefore will resemble those of the West. But what one hopes is that, over and above all this, the 'soul' of each country will remain unchanged and resemble only itself; that the African of tomorrow will be able to go on recognizing himself in the African of yesterday, the Indian of tomorrow in his brothers of past centuries. It is not for any one of us to lay down the conditions in which, across eternity, this would be possible. And yet ... And yet, I should like at least to indicate some of the elements of the problem as it presents itself to me in India.

Namaskar

There is no Hindu humanism in the sense in which we use that word in the West. There is Hindu culture, which is far from primitive, a world in itself, into which one cannot plunge without getting dizzy; but that culture is not the culture of man. At the caste level the group is prized at the expense of the individual; at the level of the Absolute, the individual no longer exists, he is resorbed into total non-differentiation; sometimes as a link in the uninterrupted chain of rebirths, sometimes as a sort of ephemeral spark which is rapidly fused with the eternal light of Brahman. Nowhere is man the centre of Hindu speculative thought, nowhere has he any value in himself. One could say that at the present time the essential face of India, and that which it prefers to show to the world, is the aspect of being in perpetual flight towards the Absolute; and it is this which may well survive the caste system of society.

But at the same time there is the new economic and social life growing up outside these perspectives, establishing new relations between men and, in particular, working relations where they are bound to discover their real human face, their solidarity – professional, class, or simply human – and their responsibility as citizens. In short, man will little by little become the centre of interest, the source of and standard for all values; the new ethical framework which will replace the ancient one will then perhaps be very much more like ours than at present or in the past.

How will the Hindu – the Indian – deal with these new attainments on the plane of speculative thought? Will he integrate them, as he previously integrated caste, in his vision of the one and paramount Brahman? Will man, in his new form, be thrown back into cosmic illusion? Or, on the contrary, will the new core of values prove too resistant, too real? In any case, it would refuse to let itself be absorbed in the unity of everything, and it is this which throws it back into illusion. Non-differentiation would then no longer be the point of arrival, but, from the very start, the chaos out of which man must organize cosmos. And such a man would then raise himself to the heights of a demiurge – a vision which would also be much closer to our own than the present one.

But it is very hard to answer a question of this kind.

May I take leave?

A Small Vocabulary for the Reader and the Tourist

I have given the vocabulary of religion separately; it is by far the larger, probably because Indian ideas often do not have a simple equivalent in our language. The division between the secular and the religious was not really necessary, but it has at least avoided sandwiching dharma between the coolie and the washerman.

Ahimsâ	Non-violence.
Anjali	A gesture of worship which consists of joining the hands vertically at about the level of the face.
Ashram	A Hindu hermitage or monastery centred round the person of the guru.
Avatâr	'Descent': ·the term is generally applied to Vishnu's manifestations in the world. The more common translation 'incarnation', is not strictly correct since the god only appears to be vested with mortal attributes. Krishna is the most venerated of Vishnu's avatars.
Bhajan	Religious singing generally in honour of Krishna, either in the temple or before the domestic altar.
Bhikshu	'Beggar': name for the Buddhist monk who may live only by begging alms.
Brahman	The Absolute in its perfect form.
Dharma	The sacred law of the universe which determines cosmic order as well as human order. It is thus also the moral and religious law for man, which differs according to caste.
Guru	A spiritual teacher. Usually nowadays a religious hermit, surrounded by his disciples, whom he instructs in the ways of arriving at mystical experience. By tradition it is the Brahman versed in the Scriptures to whom young Brahmanical students are sent so that he may pass on to them his knowledge of sacred texts.
Gurukul	'The Guru's family.' It includes, besides the Brahman-Guru's own family, the disciples studying under him and giving service in return for his teaching. It is also the name given, because of the traditionalist inspiration which animates them, to the schools founded by the Arya-Samaj.
Linga	Cylindrical stone symbolizing Siva.
Mantra	A magic formula or prayer.
Moksha or Mukti	'Liberation.' The word for ultimate salvation, the escape from the cycle of rebirths.
Pûjâ	Religious ceremony performed before the image of god by a priest in a temple or by the head of the family in the home. It has a more devotional than sacrificial character.
Rishi	'Seer' of ancient times who was able to perceive by intuition the religious law, dharma, as later transmitted in the sacred writings.
Rita	An older name for dharma.
Sâdhu	'Saint.' Wandering ascetic, living alone or in bands. He may belong to this or that religious sect, but is recognized as a rule by his saffron-coloured garb.
Samsâra	The cycle of rebirths.·
Sannyâsi	The Brahman who, having been the head of a household and father of a family, renounces everything and lives as a hermit. Today the term is more or less interchangeable with sadhu.
Shâstra	Generic term for the treatises on traditional and sacred knowledge, from phonetics and grammar to dancing and architecture, taking in such subjects as medicine and the art of love-making.

Shramana	The ascetic, possibly of Jainist origin. Identified by some people with the shaman of Central Asia.
Shuddhi	Purity, cleanness.
Siddha	'The perfect,' he who has 'realized' the identity of self and the universal Self of the Absolute.
Yogi	He who, to attain supreme knowledge, practises yoga exercises. N.B. Not to be confused with the fakirs, who are exportable commodities for the use of Westerners, and whom one is not likely to encounter in India outside the big tourist hotels and at fairs, where they take their place beside snake-charmers.
Acchâ	Good, that's all right.
Brahman	Member of the highest, priestly caste.
Chapati	Sort of pancake made of flour and water which is the staple diet of the Indians in the Northern plain.
Coolie	From a Tamil word — kuli — meaning wage. The coolie is the odd-job man, the station porter, the hall porter, and so on.
Dhobi	Washerman.
Dhoti	A sort of skirt falling to the feet, worn by men.
Ghat	Steps leading down to a river or pool where people bathe and do their washing. Also name given by Europeans to mountain ranges parallel to the East and West coasts of India.
Kshatriya	Member of the second, warrior and princely caste.
Lota	Small copper or brass cup which the Hindu carries about wherever he goes. A sort of portable shower.
Memsahib	Madam.
Mleccha	Barbarian. Used to designate anyone outside Hindu society, which itself includes people of caste and out-castes.
Pandit	Brahman versed in traditional knowledge.
Pardah	Custom of Muslim origin — like the word itself — which consists of forbidding women to go out unless veiled or behind curtains to hide them from male eyes.
Pariah	Name of a caste of Untouchables in southern India who are tambourine-players at funerals. It has come to be applied in a general way to all Untouchables, in which sense it is used only by Europeans.
Sahib	Sir.
Sari	Women's dress, with local variations.
Shikhara	Elongated cone-shaped roof covering the sanctuary of temples in the North.
Shûdra	Member of the fourth Hindu caste, that of servants and artisans who are not untouchable.
Vaishya	Member of the third caste, that of farmers and tradesmen.

The language of gestures: a movement of the head meaning 'no' is, more or less as with us, a slight rolling of the head from side to side, while to indicate 'yes', or to show that he has understood, the Indian gives an inimitable shake of the head at the level of the shoulders. To beckon someone, you make a movement as though picking up a ball from a billiard-table, with the arm extended at full length. The small gesture of the finger familiar to us is not understood anywhere in India.

To this should be added a few English words which have lost their original meaning. Such as 'bearer', who bears nothing; he is the personal servant who does the shopping and the cooking, but calls a coolie if there is luggage to be carried; 'sweeper', who does not sweep but cleans out the latrines daily.

money

India had a system of money and of weights and measures about as simple as the British. But in an attempt to modernize itself it introduced the decimal system.

1 rupee = 16 annas; 1 anna = 4 paisa (old currency) = 100 Paisa. (naya paisa, new smallest denomination).
(The rupee is worth 1/6 $ 0.21).

some books

B A S H A M, A. L. — The Wonder that was India.
B I N A N I, G. D. & R A M A R A O, T. V. — India at a Glance.
C A M E R O N, R. — Shadows deom India.
F O R S T E R, E. M. — A Passage to India.
G R I F F I T H S, P. — Modern India.
                      The British in India.
G O P U L A N, A. K. — Kerala, Past and Present.
L E W I S, J. — The Religions of the World Made Simple.
M O R E L A N D, W. H. & C H A T T E R J E E, A. C. — A Short History of India.
N E H R U, J. — Discovery of India.

photographs

Martine Wilmark archives, pp. 1, 2—3, 21, 39, 40, 85, 137, 179, 180, 191. — Marc Riboud-Magnum, pp. 4, 32a, 88, 110, 115, 118, 119, 185. — Henri Cartier-Bresson-Magnum, pp. 49, 70, 71, 86, 95, 112. — Werner Bischof-Magnum, pp. 53, 90, 104, 140, 151. — Denis Brihat-Rapho, pp. 6, 17, 42, 54, 56, 60, 69, 72, 75, 83, 92, 121, 122, 128, 138, 140, 143, 164, 175, 181. — Louis Frédéric-Rapho, pp. 2 cv., 11, 13, 36, 47, 51, 77, 78, 99, 120, 127, 154, 155, 157, 158, 168, 169, 182. — Gabriel Terrier, pp. 29, 31, 59, 62, 73, 81, 111, 131, 145, 186, 188. — Roger Viollet, pp. 22, 23, 26, 57, 82, 100, 161, 171, 173. — Atlas Photo, p. 41. — Keystone, p. 135. — Cahiers du Cinéma, p. 32b. — Bibliothèque Nationale, pp. 9, 10, 15, 87, 139. — India Tourist Office, pp. 52, 55, 107.
The cover picture is by Marc Riboud.

This book was designed under the supervision of Juliette Caputo.

Printed by N.V. Grafische Industrie Haarlem — Holland